# GET BY IN

# ITALIAN

# A QUICK BEGINNER'S COURSE FOR
# HOLIDAYMAKERS AND BUSINESS PEOPLE

### EMMANUELA TANDELLO

BBC BOOKS

## ACKNOWLEDGEMENTS

The author and producer wish to thank all those who contributed to the production of the book and cassettes for *Get by in Italian*. In particular, we would like to thank our local co-ordinator, Francesca Puchetti, and those people whose voices are heard more often on the cassettes: Giulia Puchetti, Sergio and Isabella Tamburini, Paola Putti-Sinigaglia, Margherita Coeli-Simonato, Franco Borghesan, Attilio Germano, Stefano Zanetti and Michele Tandello.

Many thanks for their valuable help to: Rosanna Longo at the IAT office in Padua; the owners and personnel of Ristorante 'Al Pero' in Padua, and Trattoria Ristorante 'Al Castelletto da Taparo' in Torreglia; Zanetti Group, and the personnel at Padua Railway Station.

For the studio-production in England: Martin Dyster of Thatched Cottage Studio; Rosemary Plum, presenter, Alberto Janelli and Anna Mazzotta, actors.

Thanks also to Emanuela Davey for the transcripts of the site recordings and to Alan Wilding for all the improvements he suggested.

EMMANUELA TANDELLO & STEPHANIE RYBAK

*Published by BBC Books*
a division of BBC Enterprises Ltd, Woodlands
80 Wood Lane, London W12 0TT
First published 1992, © Emmanuela Tandello 1992
General Editor: Alan Wilding
Reprinted 1992
The moral rights of the author have been asserted
ISBN 0 563 36145 X
Designed by Peter Bridgewater
Map and illustrations by Lorraine Harrison
Cover illustration by Tony Masero
Set in Great Britain by
Central Southern Typesetters, Eastbourne
Printed and bound in Great Britain by Clays Ltd, St Ives plc
Cover printed by Clays Ltd, St Ives plc
Exclusive U.S. Distributor of the Get By in Series Packs
Ambrose Video Publishing Inc.
1290 Avenue of the Americas, Suite 2245
New York, N.Y. 10104

# CONTENTS

## INTRODUCTION

The new BBC *Get by in Italian* is a six unit course for anyone planning a visit to Italy, whether for pleasure or business. It aims to provide the basic language and information for some of the most common situations of a visit abroad.

The course consists of a book and two 90 minute cassettes, to be used *together*. Each unit deals with specific areas of conversation: saying hello, shopping, travelling around, getting somewhere to stay, eating out, meeting people and doing business.

The *Get by* book includes:
- the key words and phrases for each unit;
- the texts of the recorded dialogues in the order they'll be heard on the cassettes;
- notes on each dialogue and a section at the end of each unit giving explanations of the language met; you will need to refer forward to these explanations in order to do some of the exercises;
- background information worth knowing about Italy and Italian customs;
- self-checking exercises for you to do between dialogues, and at the end of each unit (*Can you get by?*).

   (When you come across the cassette only exercise symbol, listen to your tape for your instructions, *and* for your answer, as it will not always appear in the key).
- a short reference section or appendix containing a guide to the basics of Italian pronunciation and extra language notes;
- the keys to the exercises and the transcripts of the listening exercises that you'll hear on the cassettes;
- a word list.

The *Get by* cassettes contain all the dialogues, help with the language used in them, and listening and speaking exercises. They give you plenty of opportunity to practise all the key words and phrases at your own pace. Words which are introduced on the tape can be found in the Explanations section of the same unit.

To make the most of the course:

- The book and cassettes are designed to be used together. But, of course, you can reinforce what you have learnt by re-listening to the cassettes while driving, for example.

- The following symbols stand for book only ☐☐ and cassette only ☆ exercises.

- The cassette exercises and language practice have been devised to allow you as much room for repetition as possible. Pauses are left for you to repeat words and phrases and to give answers in the exercises; but winding back and listening again and repeating improves your mastery of the language – so do so as many times as you feel you want and need to! You will certainly need to listen to the dialogues several times over.

- The dialogues are authentic: they are recordings of real people using real language in real situations. There will be plenty of words you don't understand, just as there will be when you go to Italy. Don't panic! Listen out for the words that you do know, and try to understand the gist of what is being said from that. Equally, when it comes to speaking, don't worry about making mistakes; the important thing is to make yourself understood. Of course, if you've already learnt some Latin, French or Spanish, don't hesitate to guess at the Italian forms; they are usually very similar.

We wish you good luck with your Italian . . . *Buon viaggio!* . . . *e buon divertimento!*

# 1 SAYING HELLO & ORDERING DRINKS

**KEY WORDS AND PHRASES**

| | |
|---|---|
| **buongiorno** | hello, good morning |
| **ciao** | hello, hi, 'bye |
| **buonasera** | good evening |
| **arrivederci** | goodbye |
| **grazie** | thank you |
| **prego** | don't mention it |
| **sì** | yes |
| **no** | no |
| **uno, due, tre** | 1, 2, 3 |
| **quattro, cinque** | 4, 5 |
| **sei, sette** | 6, 7 |
| **otto, nove, dieci** | 8, 9, 10 |
| **per favore** | please |
| **un caffè** | a coffee |
| **un bicchiere di vino** | a glass of wine |
| **quant'è?** | how much is it? |
| **posso cambiare . . . ?** | can I change . . . ? |

### DIALOGUES

Listen to these exchanges on the cassettes:

#### SAYING HELLO AND GOODBYE

**1**

— Buongiorno.
— Buongiorno.

— Buongiorno.
— Buongiorno.
— Buongiorno.

— Buongiorno, signora.
— Buongiorno.

— Buongiorno.
— Buongiorno, signora.

*buongiorno* (literally good day) is used both to greet people and to say goodbye.
*signora* (literally madam) is more frequently used than its English equivalent.

**2**

— Buonasera!
— Buonasera!
— Buonasera!
— Buonasera!

— Buonasera, signori.
— Buonasera.
— Buonasera, dottore.

*buonasera* good evening, is the usual greeting from mid-afternoon onwards; it is used both to greet people and to say goodbye.
*signori* gentlemen; gentleman is *signore; signori,* however, is also used for ladies and gentlemen.
*dottore* doctor, though not necessarily a medical one; a title used for professional people such as engineers, solicitors, etc.

**3**

— Ciao!
— Ciao!
— Ciao!
— Ciao Isabella!

— Ciao!
— Ciao Sergio!
— Ciao Francesca!

*ciao* hello, hi! – the informal greeting used with friends and family. It also means goodbye.

**4**

— Arrivederci!        — Arrivederci!
— Arrivederci!        — Arrivederci, buongiorno.
— Arrivederci!

*arrivederci* goodbye, is used at any time of day, with anybody, and can be followed by *buongiorno* or *buonasera*.

## SAYING THANK YOU
## AND DON'T MENTION IT

**5**

— Grazie.        — Buongiorno, grazie.
— Grazie.        — Grazie, buongiorno.
— Grazie.        — Buongiorno, grazie, signora.
— Grazie, buongiorno.

**6**

— Grazie.        — Grazie.
— Prego.        — Prego.
— Grazie.        — Grazie.
— Prego.        — Prego.

*grazie* thank you
*prego* don't mention it; please is *per favore*

## LEARNING TO COUNT

**7**

— Uno, due, tre, quattro, cinque, sei, sette, otto, nove, dieci.

**8**

CATERINA       Allora! Uno . . . di' uno . . . di' uno?
                 Uno.

| | |
|---|---|
| MARIA LUISA | Uno. |
| CATERINA | Due. |
| MARIA LUISA | Due. |
| CATERINA | Tre. |
| MARIA LUISA | Tre. |
| CATERINA | Quattro . . . Quattro, prova a dire. |
| MARIA LUISA | Quattro. |
| CATERINA | Cinque . . . Di' cinque. |
| MARIA LUISA | Cinque. |
| CATERINA | Sei . . . Di' sei. |
| MARIA LUISA | Sei. |
| CATERINA | Poi sette. |
| MARIA LUISA | Sette. |
| CATERINA | Otto . . . Sai dire otto? |
| MARIA LUISA | Otto. |
| CATERINA | Nove. |
| MARIA LUISA | . . . e dieci. |
| ADULTI | . . . Nove e dieci! |

*allora* now then
*prova a dire* try to say
*di'* . . . say . . .
*poi* then
*sai dire . . . ?* can you say . . . ?
*e* and

## Exercise 1 ☆
Listen to Sergio giving his daughter some practice at
numbers. See if you can do the sums in Italian! Before you
start, two new words: *più* plus, *meno* minus. The answers are
in the Key on page 96.

## Exercise 2 ☆
Listen to the cassette and try to write down the telephone
numbers that are given.
(Transcript on page 96.)

**9**

FRANCESCA   Puoi cambiarmi diecimila lire?
ISABELLA    Sì certo. Mille, duemila, tremila, quattromila,
            cinquemila, seimila, settemila, ottomila,
            novemila, diecimila.
FRANCESCA   Grazie mille.
ISABELLA    Prego.

*puoi cambiarmi . . . ?*   can you change for me . . . ?
*certo*   certainly
*grazie mille*   thanks (literally a thousand thanks)

**10**

SERGIO      Vuole qualcosa da bere? Abbiamo limonata,
            aranciata, caffè, coca-cola, tè e acqua minerale.

*vuole . . . ?* would you like . . . ?
*qualcosa da bere* something to drink; you can adapt this phrase
to other verbs:
*qualcosa da mangiare* something to eat
*abbiamo* we have
*una limonata* lemonade
*un' aranciata* orangeade
*un caffè* coffee
*un tè* tea
*un' acqua minerale* mineral water

## ORDERING AND PAYING

### 11   A coffee

PAOLA       Buongiorno.
CAMERIERE   Buongiorno a lei.
PAOLA       Un caffè, per favore.
CAMERIERE   Un caffè . . . Pronti il caffè.
PAOLA       Grazie. Quant'è?
CAMERIERE   Novecento.

| | |
|---|---|
| PAOLA | Grazie. |
| CAMERIERE | Grazie. |

*un cameriere* a waiter; *una cameriera* a waitress
*a lei* to you; *buongiorno a lei* good day to you
*pronti il caffè* here is the coffee (*pronti* literally straight away, ready)
*quant'è?* how much is it?
*novecento* nine hundred

## 12   A cappuccino

| | |
|---|---|
| PAOLA | Un cappuccino, per favore. |
| CAMIRIERE | Un cappuccino? . . . Ecco a lei il cappuccino. |
| PAOLA | Grazie. Quant'è? |
| CAMERIERE | Milledue. |
| PAOLA | Ecco. |
| CAMERIERE | Grazie. |

*un cappuccino* is a white coffee with frothy milk on top.
*ecco a lei* here you are; *ecco* here (it) is
*milledue* 1200; the complete form should be *milleduecento,* but prices are generally given in the shortened form.

## 13   Tea, coffee and a cake

| | |
|---|---|
| PAOLA | Buongiorno. |
| CAMERIERE | Buongiorno. |
| PAOLA | Un tè al limone e un caffè lungo, per favore. |
| CAMERIERE | Va bene. Un tè al limone e un caffè . . . Ecco a lei il tè al limone e il caffè lungo. |
| PAOLA | Grazie. E una brioche e una pasta anche. |
| CAMERIERE | Ecco a lei. |
| PAOLA | Grazie. |

*un tè al limone* a lemon tea; tea with milk is *un tè al latte*
*un caffè lungo* (literally a long coffee), a weaker black coffee

*va bene* fine, OK                    *una pasta* a cake
*una brioche* a bun                   *anche* too, also

## Exercise 3 ☆
You order drinks and snacks at a café.

## 14    A coke and a beer

| | |
|---|---|
| PAOLA | Buongiorno. |
| CAMERIERE | Buongiorno. |
| PAOLA | Una coca-cola e una birra, per favore. |
| CAMERIERE | Una coca e una birra. La coca, la birra media o piccola? |
| PAOLA | Piccola, per favore. |
| CAMERIERE | Piccola . . . una birra piccola, pronti. |
| PAOLA | Grazie, quant'è? |
| CAMERIERE | Tremila. |
| PAOLA | Ecco. |
| CAMERIERE | Grazie. |

*una birra* a beer
*la birra piccola o media?* a small or medium beer?

## 15    A glass of wine

| | |
|---|---|
| PAOLA | Buongiorno. |
| CAMERIERE | Buongiorno, signora. |
| PAOLA | Un bicchiere di vino bianco e un bicchiere di vino rosso. |
| CAMERIERE | Va bene. |

*un bicchiere* a glass; *un bicchiere di vino* a glass of wine; *un bicchiere di latte* a glass of milk
*bianco* white; *rosso* red; *un bicchiere di vino bianco* a glass of white wine. Two more useful words when dealing with wine are *secco* dry, and *dolce* sweet; *un bicchiere di vino bianco secco* a glass of dry white wine.

## Exercise 4 ☆ ☐☐

Listen to the cassette. Michele asks for advice before ordering
some glasses of wine. See if you can follow enough to fill in
the following wine table:

| VINO | BIANCO | ROSSO | DOLCE | SECCO |
|------|--------|-------|-------|-------|
| *Brachetto* | | | | |
| *Soave* | | | | |

## Exercise 5 ☆

You order some drinks in a café. Listen to your tape for
instructions and answer.

## EXPLANATIONS

### SAYING HELLO AND GOODBYE

*Buongiorno* good day, and *buonasera* good evening, are used
both to greet and to say goodbye to people.

*Ciao* is used for informal greetings; with friends, or family,
but not with somebody you do not know well. Use the more
formal greetings in all shops and public places, and upon
being introduced to somebody.

*Arrivederci* means goodbye, and is used at any time, with
anybody. You can use it followed by *buongiorno,* or *buonasera;*
*Arrivederci, buongiorno.*

## NUMBERS

It is essential you should learn them thoroughly; here they are again.

| | | |
|---|---|---|
| 0 zero | | |
| 1 uno | 100 cento | 1000 mille |
| 2 due | 200 duecento | 2000 duemila |
| 3 tre | 300 trecento | 3000 tremila |
| 4 quattro | 400 quattrocento | 4000 quattromila |
| 5 cinque | 500 cinquecento | 5000 cinquemila |
| 6 sei | 600 seicento | 6000 seimila |
| 7 sette | 700 settecento | 7000 settemila |
| 8 otto | 800 ottocento | 8000 ottomila |
| 9 nove | 900 novecento | 9000 novemila |
| 10 dieci | | |

You have also come across 11, *undici*
1200 milleduecento; 2500 duemilacinquecento (sometimes in speech the *cento* is left out, so you will hear *milledue* and *duemilacinque* instead). More numbers appear on pages 44 and 94–5.

## MASCULINE AND FEMININE

Words that represent people (e.g. man, woman, waiter), or objects (money, glass, etc.) are known as nouns.

In Italian, nouns are either masculine or feminine. Masculine nouns generally end in -*o (passaporto)* and feminine ones in -*a (birra)*; nouns ending in -*e (caffè, pensione)* are less predictable. This affects the articles ('the' and 'a') that accompany the words: in the dialogues you come across *un caffè* and *una pasta*, *un tè* and *una birra*. *Un* (masc.) and *una* and *un'* (fem.) are the three words for 'a'. Adjectives (words like 'good', 'old', 'green', 'fat', 'interesting', etc.) also change according to the gender of the noun: *un vino freddo* a cold wine; *una birra fredda* a cold beer.

### *CAFFÈ, BAR*

Every Italian town possesses its own beloved old café or cafés, attractive, old-fashioned looking buildings which for centuries have been the centre of the town's public life and gossip, and have witnessed its important cultural and political events. They may be more expensive than an ordinary bar, but are well worth visiting for a real taste of Italian life.

Bars are more recent institutions. Both bars and cafés sell alcoholic and non-alcoholic drinks, coffee, tea and snacks, both sweet and savoury.

Sometimes you will have to get the receipt (*lo scontrino*) at the cash desk before going to the bar and ordering. If you sit at a table *al tavolo,* you will get waiter service, *servizio al tavolo,* and may have to pay a lot more.

The *paninoteca* (sandwich bar) is a very recent development. The name comes from *panino,* bread roll, and it is frequented mostly by the very young, who gather outside rather than inside, to sip their cokes and eat the American-style hamburgers, or the many different kinds of *panini imbottiti* (filled rolls).

If you enjoy wine and would like to find out more about it, try an *enoteca,* a connoisseur wine cellar; here you can taste many different wines, especially local ones, bearing most colourful and enticing names such as *fragolino* (strawberry-like), *dolcetto* (sweetish) and *vin santo* (holy wine).

### **DRINKS AND SNACKS**

Coffee: *un caffè espresso* is a small cup of strong black coffee.
*un caffè lungo* is slightly weaker.
*un cappuccino* is a white coffee with frothy milk.

*un caffè corretto* is a black coffee with a dash of either *grappa* or brandy.
*un caffè macchiato* is coffee with a dash of milk.

Tea: *un tè al latte* is tea with milk, but do ask for it *con latte freddo,* with cold milk, or you might be served boiled milk instead. Italians, however, prefer it *al limone,* with lemon, or, in the summer, they drink *tè freddo,* iced tea, served in a tall glass.

Chocolate: *una cioccolata calda,* hot chocolate, is generally served in the winter with whipped cream, *con panna.*

Sugar: *zucchero.*

Mineral water: *acqua minerale;* it can be either *naturale,* or *frizzante* (sparkling); you may also come across *gassata* for sparkling and *non gassata* for still.

Beer: Italian *birra* is generally lager-type, either brewed in Italy (*nazionale*) or a more expensive foreign brand (*estera*). It is always served cold.

Wine: *vino rosso* and *bianco.* Among the most famous white wines are Soave from Veneto, Tocai from Friuli and Verdicchio from Marche. Among the red ones are Barolo ('the King of wines') from Piedmont and Chianti from Tuscany.

Cakes: *una pasta* is the generic name for a small cake. In the morning it is customary to have *una brioche* with your *cappuccino;* this can contain *marmellata,* jam, or *crema,* custard cream, or it can be just plain, *normale.*

Savouries: *un salato,* or *salatino* (plural *salatini*) is an interesting change when you want a light snack: light pastry with cheese, spinach, anchovies or olives; a toasted sandwich is *un toast.*

Soft drinks: *aranciata* orangeade; *limonata* lemonade; *un frullato* a milkshake; *un succo di frutta* a fruit juice; *una spremuta* freshly squeezed fruit juice: *di limone* lemon; *di arancia* orange; *di pompelmo* grapefruit.

The exercises in this section will help you to check your progress. The answers to the exercises are on page 98–9.

**Exercise 1** ☐☐

WORD SEARCH. Can you find six expressions for greetings and thanks hideen in this puzzle? They are *buongiorno, buonasera, ciao, grazie, prego, per favore*. The puzzle works up and down, side to side and backwards.

| U | E | B | S | T | E | I | Z | A | R | G | O | M | P |
|---|---|---|---|---|---|---|---|---|---|---|---|---|---|
| L | N | U | A | R | P | C | C | D | F | H | A | N | Y |
| B | U | O | N | G | I | O | R | N | O | A | L | E | S |
| L | O | N | A | D | F | E | L | P | Q | S | U | I | T |
| O | L | A | R | T | D | D | S | O | A | F | I | L | R |
| R | I | S | T | O | P | E | R | F | A | V | O | R | E |
| Q | P | E | A | N | R | V | O | E | B | B | C | D | I |
| A | P | R | E | G | O | I | D | Z | Z | F | P | N | U |
| L | A | A | E | R | I | R | D | O | Z | P | S | V | V |
| V | L | Z | P | D | R | R | I | A | A | E | Q | P | Q |
| V | U | E | E | L | O | A | I | C | R | S | V | Z | H |

**Exercise 2** ☆ ☐☐

Bingo! Listen to the cassette, where Anna will call the numbers. Cross them out on the card below as you hear them, You should be left with one number at the end.

| 1 | | 700 | | 7 |
|---|---|---|---|---|
| | | | 900 | |
| 8000 | | 5 | | 300 |
| | 8 | | 400 | |
| 600 | | 10 | | 1000 |

**Exercise 3** ☆ ☐☐

Read the exercise first, then switch on your cassette. Give your answers aloud.

1   You want to order a glass of sweet red wine. Which will you say . . . ?

a   Un bicchiere di vino bianco dolce
b   Un bicchiere di vino rosso dolce
c   Un bicchiere di vino rosso secco

2   Now you want to order a medium-sized coke and a small beer. Which will you say . . . ?

a   Una coca piccola e una birra media
b   Una coca media e una birra piccola
c   Una coca media e una birra media

3   You want to order a coffee laced with *grappa*. Which will you ask for . . . ?

a   un caffè macchiato       c   un caffè corretto
b   un caffè lungo

**4** Now you want something to eat. Which will you say . . . ?

**a** una pasta
**b** un'aranciata
**c** una spremuta

**5** If you ask *Quant'è?,* which answer would you expect to hear . . . ?

**a** Uno, sette, cinque, otto, zero, due
**b** duemila
**c** grazie mille

# 2 SHOPPING

## KEY WORDS AND PHRASES

| | |
|---|---|
| **posso cambiare . . . ?** | can I change . . . ? |
| **un etto** | 100 grams |
| **questo** | this, this one |
| **un pezzo di . . .** | a piece of |
| **basta (così)** | that's enough |
| **Ha . . . ?** | Do you have . . . ? |
| **quanto costa?** | how much does it cost? |
| **quanto costano?** | how much do they cost? |
| **troppo caro** | too expensive |
| **posso vederlo?** | can I see it? |

## DIALOGUES

### AT THE BANK

## 1 Changing a Eurocheque

| | |
|---|---|
| FRANCESCA | Buongiorno. |
| IMPIEGATA | Buongiorno. |
| FRANCESCA | Posso cambiare un Eurocheque? |
| IMPIEGATA | Sì, certo. Al massimo di trecentomila lire. |
| FRANCESCA | Benissimo. |
| IMPIEGATA | Il suo documento? |
| FRANCESCA | Ecco. |

*un'impiegata* a female employee; *un impiegato* is a male employee

*posso* can I?, may I?; *cambiare* to change; *posso cambiare . . . ?* can I change . . . ?

*certo* certainly

*al massimo di trecentomila lire* to a maximum of 300,000 lira

*il suo* your, yours

*documento* (literally document) identification, usually a passport

*lira,* plural *lire,* is the Italian currency – see the *Worth Knowing* section in this unit

## 2   Changing a traveller's cheque

| | |
|---|---|
| STEPHANIE | Posso cambiare questo traveller's cheque, per favore? |
| IMPIEGATA | Sì, certo. È di cento sterline? |
| STEPHANIE | Sì. |
| IMPIEGATA | Bene. Il suo passaporto? |
| STEPHANIE | Ecco. |
| IMPIEGATA | Può firmare il suo traveller's cheque? |
| STEPHANIE | Ecco. |
| IMPIEGATA | Bene. Si accomodi in cassa. Arrivederci. |
| STEPHANIE | Arrivederci. Grazie, signora. |

*è* is

*di cento sterline* for a hundred pounds; *una sterlina* (pl. *sterline*) one pound sterling; *un dollaro* (pl. *dollari*) one dollar

*bene* good (literally well)

*un passaporto* passport

*può?* can you? will you please?

*firmare* to sign; *può firmare?* can you sign?

*si accomodi* in this situation is a polite way to direct you to *la cassa,* the till counter; but it is also used to show somebody in, and to get them to sit down; please sit down, make yourself comfortable.

## Exercise 1 ☆

See how well you can get by at the bank. You want to change
a Eurocheque and 100 dollars.

### BUYING FOOD

### 3   Peaches

| | |
|---|---|
| PAOLA | Buongiorno. |
| FRUTTIVENDOLO | Buongiorno. |
| PAOLA | Quattro pesche, per favore. |
| FRUTTIVENDOLO | Va bene. Tremila. |
| PAOLA | Grazie, ecco a lei. |

*il fruttivendolo* the fruitseller
*pesche* peaches (sing. *una pesca*)

### 4   Bread rolls

| | |
|---|---|
| PAOLA | Buongiorno. |
| NEGOZIANTE | Buongiorno. |
| PAOLA | Quattro panini, per favore. |
| NEGOZIANTE | Sì, subito . . . vuole normali? |
| PAOLA | Sì, questi, per favore. |
| NEGOZIANTE | Basta così? |
| PAOLA | Basta così, grazie. |
| NEGOZIANTE | Sei e cinquanta. |

*un, una negoziante* shopkeeper
*un panino* a bread roll
*normale* ordinary
*vuole?* would you like?
*questi* these
*basta così* it is enough, that's all

### 5   200 grams of ham

| | |
|---|---|
| SALUMIERE | Buongiorno, signora. |

| | |
|---|---|
| MARGHERITA | Buongiorno. |
| SALUMIERE | Mi dica. |
| MARGHERITA | Vorrei due etti di prosciutto. |
| SALUMIERE | Cotto o crudo? |
| MARGHERITA | Cotto. Questo. |
| SALUMIERE | Va bene. |
| MARGHERITA | Bene. Quant'è? |
| SALUMIERE | Cinquemila e trecento lire. |

*il salumiere* works in *una salumeria,* selling cooked meats and
salami, and often groceries as well
*mi dica* may I help you?; you will also hear *desidera?* and *prego?*
*vorrei* I'd like; you can use this phrase with verbs, too: *vorrei
bere,* I'd like to drink. Another phrase for ordering is: *mi
dà . . . ?* will you give me . . . ?
*un etto* 100 grams
*il prosciutto* ham
*cotto* cooked; *crudo* raw (i.e. cured, like Parma ham)

## 6  Cheese

| | |
|---|---|
| MARGHERITA | Ha del formaggio? |
| SALUMIERE | No, mi dispiace. |
| MARGHERITA | Va bene, grazie. |

## 7

| | |
|---|---|
| GIULIA | Buongiorno. |
| SALUMIERE | Buongiorno. |
| GIULIA | Vorrei un pezzo di parmigiano, per favore. |
| SALUMIERE | Quanto? |
| GIULIA | Un etto. |
| SALUMIERE | Basta così? |
| GIULIA | Sì, grazie. |
| SALUMIERE | Dopo? |
| GIULIA | Basta, grazie. |
| SALUMIERE | Grazie a lei, molto gentile . . . |

*Ha . . . ?* do you have?
*del formaggio* any/some cheese?
*no, mi dispiace* I am afraid not
*un pezzo di parmigiano* a piece of parmesan (this cheese is generally grated at home). If you want to say a little of, the expression is *un po' di*
*quanto?* how much? how many is *quanti?*
*dopo* (literally) afterwards. Here are two other questions you will regularly be asked in shops; *altro?* anything else? *poi?* then?
*basta, grazie* that's all, thanks
*molto gentile* very kind of you

## Exercise 2 ☆
You are buying some ham, some cheese and some butter (*il burro*).

## 8 Ice cream

| PAOLA | Buongiorno. |
|---|---|
| GELATAIO | Buongiorno, signorina. |
| PAOLA | Un gelato, per piacere. |
| GELATAIO | Un gelato, sì. Che gusto desidera? |
| PAOLA | (*pointing*) Eh, questo qui. |
| GELATAIO | Questo qui, eh, al limone? |
| PAOLA | Sì, grazie. |
| GELATAIO | Al limone. Pronti il gelato. |
| PAOLA | Quant'è? |
| GELATAIO | Mille. |
| PAOLA | Ecco. |
| GELATAIO | Grazie, arrivederci. |
| PAOLA | Buongiorno, grazie. |

the *gelataio* works in *una gelateria* and sells *gelati* ice creams
*signorina* miss – now generally used with very young women
*un gelato* an ice cream

*per piacere* please (an alternative to *per favore*)
*che gusto?* what flavour?
*desidera* would you like
*questo qui* this one here

## Exercise 3 ☆

Listen to another *gelataio* listing the flavours he sells. See if you can catch whether he sells peach-flavoured ice cream and chocolate ice cream. (Transcript on page 99.)

### AT THE CHEMIST'S

**9**

| | |
|---|---|
| PAOLA | Buongiorno. |
| FARMACISTA | Buongiorno, signora. |
| PAOLA | Ha qualcosa per la diarrea? |
| FARMACISTA | Sì, queste gocce. Quindici tre volte al giorno. |
| PAOLA | Benissimo. Quant'è? |
| FARMACISTA | Eh . . . sono seimilanovecentocinquanta lire. |
| PAOLA | Ecco a lei. |
| FARMACISTA | Grazie. |

*a farmacista* chemist works in a *farmacia* chemist's shop
*qualcosa per . . .* something for . . . ; *ha qualcosa per la diarrea?*
do you have anything for diarrhoea?
*gocce* (sing. *goccia*) drops
*quindici* fifteen
*volte* times
*al giorno* per day; *tre volte al giorno* three times a day
*benissimo* very good (literally very well)
*sono seimilanovecentocinquanta lire* it is 6,950 lire

## AT THE TOBACCONIST'S
. . . . . . . . . . . . . . . . . . . . . . . . . . .

### 10  Buying *gettoni*

| | |
|---|---|
| PAOLA | Buongiorno. |
| NEGOZIANTE | Buongiorno. |
| PAOLA | Ha dei gettoni, per favore? |
| NEGOZIANTE | Sì, certo, quanti? |
| PAOLA | Uno. |
| NEGOZIANTE | Eh, ecco, tenga. |
| PAOLA | Quant'è? |
| NEGOZIANTE | Eh, duecento. |
| PAOLA | Ecco a lei. |
| NEGOZIANTE | Grazie. |
| PAOLA | Grazie, buongiorno. |
| NEGOZIANTE | Buongiorno. |

*un gettone* (pl. *gettoni*) a telephone token; *dei gettoni* some/any
telephone tokens
*ecco tenga* here it is (literally here, take it)

### 11  Buying a phone card

| | |
|---|---|
| PAOLA | Buongiorno. |
| NEGOZIANTE | Buongiorno. |
| PAOLA | Ha delle carte telefoniche? |
| NEGOZIANTE | Sì. Da cinquemila, o da diecimila lire? |
| PAOLA | Una da cinquemila, per favore. |
| NEGOZIANTE | Ecco. |
| PAOLA | Grazie, buongiorno. |
| NEGOZIANTE | Buongiorno, grazie. |

*carta telefonica* (pl. *carte telefoniche*) a phone card; *delle carte
telefoniche* some, any phone cards
*da* expresses value; *da cinquemila* a five thousand lire (phone
card)

## 12   Buying stamps

| | |
|---|---|
| TABACCAIO | Buongiorno. Prego? |
| GIULIA | Buongiorno. Quanto costano i francobolli per lettera per l'Inghilterra? |
| TABACCAIO | Settecento lire per lettera. |
| GIULIA | E cartolina? |
| TABACCAIO | Seicento. |
| GIULIA | Venti francobolli per lettera per l'Inghilterra. |
| TABACCAIO | Allora, dieci e . . . venti. Quattordicimila. |
| GIULIA | Quattordici . . . ho ventimila. |
| TABACCAIO | Ecco, seimila di resto. |
| GIULIA E TABACCAIO | Grazie. |

*il tabaccaio* the tabacconist; he works in *una tabaccheria.*
*quanto costano . . . ?* how much do (the stamps) cost?
*un francobollo* (pl. *francobolli*) is a stamp; they are sold *per lettera,*
for letters, and *per cartolina,* for postcards
*venti* twenty
*quattordici* fourteen
*Ho* I have
*(seimila) di resto* (six thousand) change

### Exercise 4 ☆
You buy telephone tokens, a phone card and stamps.

### AT THE SHOPS
. . . . . . . . . . . . . . . . . . . . . . . . . . . . . .

## 13   Buying a present

| | |
|---|---|
| PAOLA | Buongiorno. |
| NEGOZIANTE | Buongiorno, signorina. |
| PAOLA | Quanto costa questo portafoglio? |
| NEGOZIANTE | Questo portafoglio costa ottantacinque-mila lire. |
| PAOLA | Uhm . . . troppo caro. Ha qualcosa di . . . meno caro? |

| | |
|---|---|
| NEGOZIANTE | Sì, ho questo sempre in pelle e costa trentacinquemila lire. Oppure qualcosina che costa venticinque. |
| PAOLA | Posso vederlo? |
| NEGOZIANTE | Certo. |
| PAOLA | Va bene questo. |
| NEGOZIANTE | Bene. Le faccio un pacchettino? |
| PAOLA | No, grazie . . . Ecco venticinque. |
| NEGOZIANTE | Benissimo. Grazie. |
| PAOLA | Buongiorno, grazie. |
| NEGOZIANTE | Arrivederci, buongiorno. |

*quanto costa questo portafoglio?* how much does this wallet cost? You can also use *quanto costa?* on its own to mean how much does it cost?

*ottantacinquemila* 85,000

*troppo* too, too much

*caro* dear, expensive

*qualcosa* something; *qualcosa di meno caro* something less expensive; another useful expression is *qualcosa di più grande,* something bigger

*sempre* still

*in pelle* in leather

*trentacinquemila* 35,000

*oppure* or (else)

*qualcosina* (the diminutive form of *qualcosa*) a little something

*venticinque* twenty-five

*posso vederlo?* may I see it? *vederlo* is a compound word formed of *vedere* to see, and *lo* it

*le* for you

*Le faccio un pacchettino?* Shall I gift-wrap it? *faccio* comes from *fare* to do or to make

*un pacchettino* is a diminutive for *pacchetto* (package)

## EXPLANATIONS

### *IL* AND *LA*

*il*, *l'* and *lo* (masc.) and *la* and *l'* (fem.) are the Italian
equivalents of 'the'. *il* is used with most masculine words: *il
panino* the bread roll, *il telefono* the telephone. For masculine
nouns beginning *sc. . ., st. . ., sp. . ., ps. . .* and *z* use *lo: lo
scontrino* the receipt, *lo zucchero*.
*la* is used with most feminine words: *la pesca* the peach, *la carta*
the card.
*l'* is used for both masculine and feminine nouns beginning
with a vowel: *l'aranciata* orangeade, *l'etto* 100 grams.
The plural of *il* is *i: i francobolli* the stamps, *i documenti* the
documents. The plural of *lo* is *gli: gli scontrini* the receipts.
The plural of *la* is *le: le lettere* the letters, *le cartoline* the
postcards.

### *DEL* AND *DELLA*

*del* and *della* mean some, any: *Ha del formaggio?* Do you have
any cheese? *della limonata?* any lemonade? *Ha della birra?* Do
you have any beer?
The plural of *del* is *dei: Ha dei francobolli?* Do you have any
stamps? *Ha dei gettoni?* Do you have any tokens?
The plural of *della* is *delle: delle lettere* some letters; *Ha delle carte
telefoniche?* Do you have any phone cards?

### PLURALS

You have come across the plurals of some nouns already: *lire,
pesche, panini . . .* In general, the masculine plural ends in *-i; il
panino, i panini*. The feminine plural usually ends in *-e: la
cartolina, le cartoline*.
Some words, particularly foreign words used in Italian, do
not change in the plural; *caffè* is one of them, and so is *bar: i
caffè, i bar*.

### QUESTO, QUESTA

*questo, questa* is the word for 'this' and, like other adjectives, it changes according to whether the word it refers to is masculine or feminine, singular or plural: *questo portafoglio* (masc.) this wallet; *questa pasta* (fem.) this cake; *questi panini* (masc. pl.) these bread rolls; *queste pesche* (fem. pl.) these peaches.

### QUANTO COSTA? QUANTO COSTANO?

*costare* means to cost. *costa* is the singular form: *questo portafoglio costa ottantacinquemila lire* this wallet costs 85,000 lire; *costano* is the plural form: *queste pesche costano tremila al chilo* these peaches cost 3,000 lire per kilo.
*quant'è?* and *quanto costa?* are more or less interchangeable, like 'How much is it?' and 'How much does it cost?' in English.

### DA

*da* expresses value: *una carta telefonica da cinquemila* a five thousand lire phone card; it is used with notes *banconote,* and coins *monete: una banconota da diecimila lire,* a ten thousand lire note; *una moneta da cinquecento lire* a five hundred lire coin.

### WORTH KNOWING

### BANKS

Banks in Italy are open from Monday to Friday, generally between 8.30 in the morning until 1.30 in the afternoon. To change currency look for the sign *Cambio*. If you wish to change a Eurocheque you will need to show your Eurocheque card and your passport. The clerk will probably take a photocopy of the first two pages of your passport; this is common practice, and should not alarm you! There may also be a small charge (*il bollo*). You may also be asked where you are staying: *Dove abita?* You only need to reply with the name of your hotel.

Most Italian banks are equipped with express service tills working 24 hours a day, which accept most Visa cards. Other places where you can change money are the *Aziende di Promozione Turistica* (APT), to be found in all main railway stations, and at tourist information centres (*Informazioni Turistiche*); as well as at the *Uffici Cambio* (exchange offices). These have different opening times, so beware!

## MONEY

The Italian currency is the *lira* (written £, like the pound sterling), plural *lire*. Banknotes (*banconote*) come in denominations of 1,000, 2,000, 5,000, 10,000, 20,000, 50,000, and 100,000 lire. The main coins are 50, 100, 200, 500 and 1,000 *lire*.

## POSTAL SERVICES

The main post office in Italy is called *Poste e Telecomunicazioni*. The initials PT appear on the notice marking an individual post office, *ufficio postale*. *L'ufficio postale* is generally open between 8.15 am and 1.30 pm from Mondays to Fridays; 8.15 am and 12.20 pm on Saturdays. Post boxes are generally red, and bear two different slots; *per la città,* for local mail, and *per tutte le altre destinazioni,* for all other destinations. There are different postal rates in Italy: *per lettera,* for letters, and *per cartolina,* for postcards. You can get stamps also from tobacconists', easily recognizable by their distinctive notice: a large white T. Italians tend to subsume the whole of the United Kingdom under *Inghilterra,* England. People therefore generally ask for *francobolli per l'Inghilterra,* even when they are sending letters to John O'Groats. If you want to be precise, you should ask for *un francobollo per la Gran Bretagna.*

## SHOPS

*farmacia* is the chemist's shop. Chemists are open Monday to Friday. If you need a chemist at the weekend, or during the night, you will find the emergency rota (headed *farmacie di turno*) on the door of most chemists' shops.

Here is a list of the most common ailments, and how to ask for something to cure them; *ha qualcosa per . . . ?*

*il mal di testa* headache
*il mal di stomaco* stomach–ache
*il mal di denti* toothache
*il raffreddore* a cold

For some ailments, instead of tablets (*compresse*) you will be given *gocce,* drops, to be taken at regular intervals.

*alimentari* local grocer's shop

*panetteria* baker's, sells bread, flour, cakes and biscuits

*pasticceria* patisserie

*mercato* market

*supermercato* supermarket

*frutta e verdura* is the greengrocer's. Here is a list of produce you may want to buy:

| | |
|---|---|
| *mele* apples | *fragole* strawberries |
| *banane* bananas | *pomodori* tomatoes |
| *arance* oranges | *peperoni* peppers |
| *pere* pears | *carote* carrots |
| *pompelmi* grapefruit | *patate* potatoes |

You will probably want to buy these by the kilo or half-kilo: *un chilo, mezzo chilo macelleria* butcher's shop

*cantina* wine shop

*profumeria* the perfumery, also sells cosmetics

*valigeria* leather-goods shop; a handbag is *una borsetta* and a belt is *una cintura*.

### TELEPHONES

In Italy you can telephone from a public phone (*telefono pubblico*), from a bar, or from a hotel. If you are calling from your hotel room, you may have to ask to be given the line: *mi dà la linea?* can you give me the line?

Public phones take *gettoni* tokens, and/or coins: 100, 200, and 500 lire. Many also take *una carta telefonica* a phone card. You can get these, too, from a tobacconist.

The code for international calls is 00, followed by the code of the country (44 for Britain, 1 for the United States), then the code of the town or village (without the 0), and then the telephone number of the person you wish to call. So, to call the British number 0123 456789 from Italy, you would dial 00 44 123 456789.

Italian numbers, after the code (*il prefisso*) have between five and seven digits; generally each digit is said individually, but sometimes people will couple them: *cinquanta* (50), *venti* (20) *undici* (11), 0 is *zero*.

Phone calls can be local, national (*teleselezione nazionale*) or international (*teleselezione internazionale*); 113 is the emergency number for police, ambulance, fire service, etc.

### CAN YOU GET BY?

### Exercise 1 ☆
See whether you can memorise Anna's shopping list!

**Exercise 2** ☆
Some practice at understanding prices. (Transcript on page 99.)

**Exercise 3** ☆ ☐ ☐
Read the exercise, and then work through it with the tape.

1   You are buying a present. Which will you say?
a   Vuole un portafoglio?
b   Vorrei un portafoglio.
c   Abbiamo un portafoglio.

2   You want to ask how much it costs. Will you say . . . ?
a   Quanto costano?
b   Quanto costa?
c   Questo qui?

3   You want to ask if they have something less expensive. Which will you say . . . ?
a   Ha qualcosa di meno grande?
b   Ho ventimila.
c   Ha qualcosa di meno caro?

4   You would like to see the cheaper wallet. Which will you say . . . ?
a   Posso cambiare?
b   Può firmare?
c   Posso vederlo?

5   How will you say 'This one's fine'?
a   Sì, certo. Quanti?
b   Va bene questo.
c   Cotto. Questo.

# 3 TRAVELLING AROUND

## KEY WORDS AND PHRASES

| | |
|---|---|
| **scusi?** | excuse me? |
| **dov'è?** | where is? |
| **ha una pianta della città?** | do you have a map of the town? |
| **per andare a . . . ?** | the way to . . . ? |
| **può ripetere?** | can you repeat, please? |
| **a destra** | to the right |
| **a sinistra** | to the left |
| **dritto** | straight on |
| **non ho capito** | I have not understood |
| **quale autobus?** | which bus? |
| **dove posso trovare i biglietti?** | where can I get the tickets? |
| **due biglietti per . . .** | two tickets for . . . |
| **un'andata** | a single (ticket) |
| **un'andata e ritorno** | a return ticket |
| **prima classe** | first class |
| **seconda classe** | second class |
| **da che binario parte?** | from which platform does it leave? |
| **a che ora?** | at what time? |

## DIALOGUES

### ASKING THE WAY

**1**

| | |
|---|---|
| GIULIA | Mi scusi, dov'è la toilette? |
| ALBERGATRICE | Al secondo piano. |
| GIULIA | Grazie. |
| ALBERGATRICE | Prego. |

*albergatrice* hotelier (fem.)
*mi scusi . . . ?* excuse me . . . ? You can also simply say *scusi . . . ?*
*dov'è . . . ?* where is . . . ?
*la toilette* the toilet
*al secondo piano* on the second floor; on the first floor is *al primo piano*

**2**

| | |
|---|---|
| FRANCESCA | Buongiorno. |
| IMPIEGATA | Buongiorno, signora. |
| FRANCESCA | Ha una pianta della città, per favore? |
| IMPIEGATA | Sì, eccola. Noi siamo qui in stazione; questo è il centro storico di Padova. |
| FRANCESCA | Dov'è il Duomo? |
| IMPIEGATA | È qui. |
| FRANCESCA | Grazie mille. |
| IMPIEGATA | Prego. |

*Ha una pianta della città?* Do you have a street-map of the city?
*eccola* here it is (*la* refers to *la pianta*)
*noi siamo qui* we are here; she is pointing at the map.
*in stazione* at the station
*il centro storico di Padova* the historical centre of Padua
*il Duomo* the cathedral

## Exercise 1 ☆ ☐ ☐

Here are the names for some major cities. The presenter on the cassette will prompt you to ask for a map for some of them. For example: 'Do you have a street-map of Padua?' is *Ha una pianta di Padova?*

| | | | |
|---|---|---|---|
| *Torino* | Turin | *Venezia* | Venice |
| *Milano* | Milan | *Firenze* | Florence |
| *Genova* | Genoa | *Roma* | Rome |
| *Padova* | Padua | *Napoli* | Naples |

See page 4 for a map of Italy.

### 3

| | |
|---|---|
| FRANCESCA | Scusi, dov'è la fiera? |
| IMPIEGATA | Allora, fuori della stazione, a sinistra, sempre dritto; dopo il semaforo sempre dritto e subito a sinistra. |
| FRANCESCA | Grazie mille. |
| IMPIEGATA | Prego. |

*la fiera* the trade fair
*fuori della stazione* outside the station
*a sinistra* on the left
*sempre dritto* straight on
*dopo il semaforo* after the lights
*subito a sinistra* immediately left

### 4

| | |
|---|---|
| STEPHANIE | Scusi, per andare a Santa Giustina, per favore? |
| GIULIA | Vada dritto, giri a sinistra, vada sempre dritto; dopo il semaforo, continui sempre dritto e sulla destra trova Santa Giustina. |

*per andare a Santa Giustina?* to go to (the church of) Santa Giustina?

| | |
|---|---|
| *vada dritto* go straight on | *sulla destra* on the right |
| *giri a sinistra* turn left | *trova* you find |
| *continui* continue on | |

**5**

Listen to Stephanie on the cassette asking the way to Vicenza. See if you catch whether the sign indicating the direction for Vicenza will be on the left or on the right.

| | |
|---|---|
| STEPHANIE | Scusi, per andare a Vicenza, per favore? |
| GIULIA | Vada sempre dritto, al primo semaforo giri a a destra e continui sempre dritto. A un certo punto troverà un cartello sulla sinistra che indicherà la direzione per Vicenza. |
| STEPHANIE | Può ripetere, per favore. Non ho capito. |
| GIULIA | Vada sempre dritto, al primo semaforo giri a destra, continui sempre dritto e troverà un cartello sulla sinistra che le indica la direzione per Vicenza. |
| STEPHANIE | Grazie mille. |
| GIULIA | Prego. |

*al primo semaforo* at the first lights
*a un certo punto* at one point
*troverà* you will find
*un cartello* a road sign
*che indicherà* which will indicate
*la direzione* the direction

*per Vicenza* for Vicenza
*può ripetere?* can you repeat?
*non ho capito* I have not understood
*che le indica* that shows you

### CATCHING A BUS

**6**

| | |
|---|---|
| STEPHANIE | Quale autobus va alla stazione? |
| ISABELLA | Deve prendere l'autobus numero quattro. |

*quale autobus . . . ?* which bus . . . ? *Quale autobus va alla stazione?* Which bus goes to the station?
*Deve prendere l'autobus numero quattro.* You must take the number 4 bus.

**7**

| | |
|---|---|
| FRANCESCA | Scusi, l'autobus per il centro, per favore? |
| IMPIEGATA | Sì, allora, può prendere l'autobus numero tre, otto, o il diciotto. |
| FRANCESCA | Eh, grazie. Ehm, dove posso trovare i biglietti? |
| IMPIEGATA | I biglietti, fuori della stazione, subito a destra. |
| FRANCESCA | Grazie mille. |
| IMPIEGATA | Prego. Buongiorno. |

*l'autobus per il centro* the bus for the city centre
*può prendere* you can take
*diciotto* eighteen
*dove posso trovare i biglietti?* where can I get (literally find) the tickets? a ticket is *un biglietto*.

**8**

| | |
|---|---|
| FRANCESCA | Due biglietti per l'autobus, per favore. |

### BUYING A TRAIN TICKET

**9**

— Un'andata per Bologna.
— Un'andata per Milano, per favore.

*un'andata* a single (ticket)

**10**

— Due biglietti per Verona, andata e ritorno . . . e in prima classe. Grazie.

*andata e ritorno* return (ticket)
*in prima classe* (in) first class

**11**

— Un biglietto di andata per Firenze, con supplemento rapido.

*con supplemento rapido* with supplement; *un rapido* is an Intercity train; you may have to catch one for part of your journey, in which case you must also purchase *un supplemento rapido*.

— Roma, andata e ritorno, con supplemento rapido Firenze-Roma.
— . . . Cassino, andata e ritorno, con supplemento rapido tra Pisa e Roma.

*tra* between

## Exercise 2 ☐☐

How would you say:
**a** a single to Rome, please?
**b** two return tickets to Naples, in first class.
**c** Venice, return, with a supplement for the *rapido* train.

### ASKING WHICH PLATFORM

**12**

| | |
|---|---|
| FRANCESCA | Da che binario parte il treno per Feltre? |
| IMPIEGATO | Treno per Feltre, binario nove. Treno diretto Calalzo. |
| FRANCESCA | Grazie. |
| IMPIEGATO | Prego. |

*da che binario parte il treno?* from which platform does the train leave?
*il treno per Feltre* the train to Feltre (a little Venetian town north of Venice)
*diretto* a direct line – as used here – you do not have to change train; *diretto,* however, is also a type of train (see *Worth Knowing* section for this unit).
Calalzo is the final destination of the train.

### AT WHAT TIME?
......................................

## Exercise 3 ☆

Learn how to tell the time in the *Explanations* section, and then write down the times read out by Anna and Alberto on the tape. You may also need to refer to the *More numbers* list in the same section. (Transcript on page 100.)

## 13

There is no Dialogue 13 in this unit.

## 14

| | |
|---|---|
| FRANCESCA | A che ora parte il prossimo treno per Torino? |
| IMPIEGATO | Per Torino diretto non c'è. Alle undici e venti c'è un treno per Milano con coincidenza. |
| FRANCESCA | Ah, ho capito. |

*a che ora parte . . . ?* at what time does . . . leave?
*il prossimo treno per Torino* the next train to Turin
*c'è* there is; *non c'è* there is not
*alle undici e venti* at 11.20
*con coincidenza* with a connection

## 15

| | |
|---|---|
| FRANCESCA | A che ora arriva a Torino? |
| IMPIEGATO | L'arrivo è previsto a Milano alle tredici e quarantacinque, alle quattordici e dieci la coincidenza, a Torino alle quindici e cinquantasette. |
| FRANCESCA | Grazie mille. |
| IMPIEGATO | Prego. |

*a che ora arriva a . . . ?* at what time does it arrive at . . . ?
*l'arrivo è previsto per* the arrival is scheduled for

## Exercise 4 ☐ ☆

Listen to this exercise on the tape, and fill in the blanks in the timetable with the times of departure from Milano, the connection from Bologna and arrival in Firenze.

## IL RITORNO   DA MILANO-BOLOGNA PER FIRENZE

### PARTENZA

| | | | | | | | | | | Exp | | | | | |
|---|---|---|---|---|---|---|---|---|---|---|---|---|---|---|---|
| Milano C.Le p | 0.15 | | | | | | | | | | 8.55 | 9.55 | 10.32 | | 12.45 |
| Bologna p | 2.59 | 3.37 | 5.07 | 5.42 | 6.00 | 6.08 | 6.52 | 7.42 | 7.54 | | 10.42 | 11.42 | 12.42 | 13.27 | 14.14 |

### ARRIVO

| Firenze SMN a | | 4.55 | 6.26 | 6.46 | 7.13 | | 8.27 | 8.47 | 9.06 | | 11.46 | 12.46 | 13.46 | 14.32 | |
|---|---|---|---|---|---|---|---|---|---|---|---|---|---|---|---|

## BOOKING A SEAT

### 16

| | |
|---|---|
| FRANCESCA | Vorrei un biglietto per Roma in prima classe con prenotazione. |
| IMPIEGATO | Va bene. Quando desidera partire? |
| FRANCESCA | Giovedì. |
| IMPIEGATO | Verso che ora? |
| FRANCESCA | Verso mezzogiorno. |
| IMPIEGATO | Abbiamo un rapido alle 12.59. Fumatori o non fumatori? |
| FRANCESCA | Non fumatori, grazie. |
| IMPIEGATO | Settantamila e seicento. |

*con prenotazione* with a reservation
*quando desidera partire?* when would you like to leave?
*giovedì* on Thursday
*verso che ora?* at about what time?
*mezzogiorno* midday
*fumatori o non fumatori?* smoking or non smoking?

### 17

Listen to the following announcement on the cassette; from which platform does the train for Bologna leave?

— È in partenza dal binario uno il treno diretto ventotto settantacinque delle ore dieci e cinquantasette per Terme Euganee, Monselice, Rovigo, Ferrara, Bologna/Parte dal binario uno il diretto ventotto settantacinque delle ore dieci e cinquantasette per Terme Euganee, Monselice, Rovigo, Ferrara, Bologna.

*partenza* departure; you will see the plural *partenze* on station departure boards
*È in partenza il treno diretto ventotto settantacinque* Stopping train number 2875 is on the point of departure
*ore* hours *delle ore dieci e cinquantasette* the 10.57 train
*per* for
Terme Euganee, Monselice, Rovigo and Ferrara are stations on the line between Padua and Bologna.

## EXPLANATIONS

### MORE NUMBERS

| | | | |
|---|---|---|---|
| undici | 11 | sedici | 16 |
| dodici | 12 | diciassette | 17 |
| tredici | 13 | diciotto | 18 |
| quattordici | 14 | diciannove | 19 |
| quindici | 15 | | |
| venti | 20 | venticinque | 25 |
| ventuno | 21 | ventisei | 26 |
| ventidue | 22 | ventisette | 27 |
| ventitré | 23 | ventotto | 28 |
| ventiquattro | 24 | ventinove | 29 |
| trenta | 30 | trentuno | 31 |
| quaranta | 40 | trentadue | 32, etc. |
| cinquanta | 50 | | |

*primo* first
*secondo* second
Both take the same gender as the noun: *primo piano* first floor;
*seconda classe* second class; *secondo piano* second floor.
More numbers appear on pages 15 and 94–5.

### ASKING THE WAY, *DOV'È?*

*scusi* and *mi scusi* both mean excuse me and are used for
apologising, for addressing a stranger, and for asking people
to repeat what they have said ('Sorry?'). However, 'Excuse
me', in the sense of 'May I come past please?', is *Permesso*.

*dov'è . . . ?* where is . . . ?; *dov'è la Fiera?* where is the trade
fair?; *dov'è la farmacia?* where is the chemist's shop?

*c'è* there is can be either a question: *c'è una farmacia?* is there a
chemist's?, or a statement: *c'è un rapido alle 12.10*.

*quale . . . ?* which . . . ?; *quale autobus va alla stazione?* which
bus goes to the station?; *quale treno va a Bologna?* which train
goes to Bologna?

*da quale . . . ?* from which?; *da quale binario parte il treno?*
which platform does the train leave from?

*per* for; *il treno per Bologna* the train to Bologna
*da* from; *il treno da Bologna* the train from Bologna

*dritto* straight on; *sempre dritto* is continue straight on for quite
a distance (but is often misused as an equivalent of *dritto*);
*sempre* means always.
*a sinistra* left; *a destra* right; *sulla destra* is on the right, *sulla
sinistra* on the left.
*la prima strada a destra* the first road on the right, is often
abbreviated to *la prima a destra* the first on the right.

*al semaforo* at the lights
*fino al semaforo* as far as the lights

*dopo il semaforo* after the lights
*al, fino* and *dopo* can be used with other nouns, too: *al museo* at the museum; *fino alla stazione* as far as the station; *dopo la farmacia* after the chemist's shop.

*di* of; *la pianta di Padova* the street-map of Padova; when you want to say 'of the town' though, you must say *della città*.

## IF YOU DON'T UNDERSTAND

*scusi, può ripetere?* excuse me, can you repeat that?
*non ho capito* lit. I haven't understood
*ho capito* lit. I have understood

## TELLING THE TIME

*Che ore sono?* What time is it? All hours (*le ore*) are feminine and plural: *le due, le tre, le quattro,* etc except for *l'una* one o'clock. So, *sono le due* it is two o'clock; *sono le tre* it is three o'clock; *sono le quattro* it is four o'clock, but *è l'una* it is one o'clock.

*È mezzogiorno* (masc.) it is midday
*È mezzanotte* (fem.) it is midnight
*a mezzanotte* at midnight
*da mezzanotte* from midnight
*fino a mezzanotte* until midnight

Officially, Italian time works on the basis of the 24 hour clock. Minutes are added to the hour: *le tre e venti* twenty past three; or subtracted: twenty to three is *le tre meno venti*
23.35 *le ventitré e trentacinque*
8.15 *le otto e quindici*
7.45 *le otto meno un quarto*
The expressions *un quarto* a quarter, and *mezzo/mezza* express the quarter hour and the half hour: *le dieci e un quarto* a quarter past ten; *le dieci e mezza* half past ten

| | |
|---|---|
| *mattina* morning | *domani* tomorrow |
| *pomeriggio* afternoon | *stamattina* this morning |
| *sera* evening | *oggi pomeriggio* this afternoon |
| *notte* night | *questa sera* this evening |
| *oggi* today | *dopo pranzo* after lunch |
| *ieri* yesterday | |

## WORTH KNOWING

### GETTING AROUND

**BY BUS**
*Un biglietto turistico* is a tourist ticket that gives you unlimited access to all buses for 24 hours. It can be purchased from railway stations, tourist information centres, and tobacconists'. Prices vary from city to city.

Whether you need an ordinary ticket, or a tourist one, you must purchase it before getting onto the bus.

*la fermata* is the bus stop; when at the bus terminal, generally to be found outside railway stations, look for the word *corsia* bay.

**BY TRAIN**
There are three main categories of train:
*locale* (a stopping train)
*diretto* (a slightly faster train; stopping at most stations)
*rapido* (express train); the last can be an Intercity train (abbreviated IC), or a Eurocity train (abbreviated EC). For both you need to pay a supplement, *un supplemento;* for the EC, this cannot be below a certain sum. In some cases, you must also make a reservation in advance; some IC and EC trains also carry first class only. Check these details in the timetable, *l'orario*. Look out for the words *partenze*

(departures) and *arrivi* (arrivals). Also, look out for the abbreviation RTD on the departures board; it stands for *ritardo* delay. If your train is late, the delay time will appear on the board.

You get your ticket from the *biglietteria* the ticket office.

**BY BICYCLE**

*Noleggio biciclette* In many Italian towns and cities you can hire a bicycle to get around the city centre, free of charge. The service is in fact provided by the local council, *il Comune*. You only need your passport (or any other document proving your identity). Look for the sign *Noleggio biciclette* at the railway station, or ask at the information centre. There may be several hiring points in the centre of town, too.

Two major offices will give you all the information you need about the city or town you are visiting: the *APT* offices (*Azienda di Promozione Turistica*), and the *IAT* offices (*Uffici di Informazione ed Assistenza Turistica*). The latter are to be found in all railway stations.

One last useful expression: *Buon viaggio!* Bon voyage!

## CAN YOU GET BY?

### Exercise 1 ☆
Listen to the recording of the switchboard operator giving you the opening times of an office. Between what times is it open in the afternoon? (Transcript on page 100.)

### Exercise 2 ☐☐
Buying tickets for buses and trains

1   You want to buy a bus ticket for the city centre. Which will you say?

**a**   Due biglietti, per favore        **c**   L'autobus per il centro,
**b**   Un biglietto, per favore                per favore?

**2** You want to ask which stop the bus leaves from. Which will you say?

**a** Da che binario parte?

**b** Dov'è il centro storico?

**c** Da che fermata parte?

**3** You want to buy a train ticket, 2nd class, return, to Milan. Which will you say?

**a** Un'andata in seconda classe per Milano.

**b** Un biglietto di andate e ritorno, seconda classe, per Milano.

**c** Uno per Milano, per favore.

**4** You want to leave today, at about two o'clock. Which will you say?

**a** Oggi, verso mezzogiorno.

**b** Domani, verso le due.

**c** Oggi, verso le due.

## Exercise 3 ☆ ☐ ☐

Complete the following dialogue.

| | |
|---|---|
| YOU | A single to Palermo in first class with a reservation. |
| IMPIEGATO | Quando desidera partire? |
| YOU | Tomorrow around midday. |
| IMPIEGATO | C'è un treno alle dodici e dieci. |
| YOU | Is there a supplement? |
| IMPIEGATO | Sì. Fumatori o non fumatori? |
| YOU | Non smoking, please. |
| IMPIEGATO | Va bene. |
| YOU | From which platform does the train leave? |
| IMPIEGATO | Dal binario numero tre. |

**Exercise 4** ☆ ☐☐

Using the map, follow the three sets of directions given on the
cassette, and see if you can work out where they are sending
you each time.

# 4 GETTING SOMEWHERE TO STAY

| | |
|---|---|
| **ha una camera libera?** | do you have a room free? |
| **una camera singola** | a single room |
| **una camera doppia** | a double room |
| **una camera matrimoniale** | a room with a double bed |
| **una camera a due letti** | a twin-bedded room |
| **con bagno** | with bathroom |
| **senza bagno** | without bathroom |
| **con doccia** | with shower |
| **la colazione** | breakfast |
| **la chiave** | the key |
| **ho prenotato** | I have booked |
| **c'è anche un ristorante?** | is there a restaurant, too? |
| **un ostello della gioventù** | youth hostel |
| **avete posto?** | do you have any room? |
| **siamo . . .** | we are . . . |
| **un campeggio** | camp-site |
| **c'è posto?** | is there any room? |
| **è all'ombra?** | is it in the shade? |

**DIALOGUES**

### BOOKING INTO A HOTEL

## A double room with bathroom
**1**

| | |
|---|---|
| SERGIO | Buonasera. |
| ALBERGATRICE | Buonasera. |
| SERGIO | Ha una camera libera? |
| ALBERGATRICE | Eh . . . sì. Che tipo di camera? |
| SERGIO | Vorrei una matrimoniale con bagno. |
| ALBERGATRICE | Sì, va bene . . . |

*ha una camera libera?* do you have a room free? The other word
for room you will come across is *una stanza.*
*che tipo di camera?* What type of room?
*una matrimoniale con bagno* a double room with bathroom;
*senza bagno* is without bathroom.

**2**

| | |
|---|---|
| ALBERGATRICE | . . . per questa notte? |
| SERGIO | Sì. Quanto viene? |
| ALBERGATRICE | Il prezzo è centoeottomila lire, esclusa la colazione. |
| SERGIO | Benissimo. |
| ALBERGATRICE | Posso avere il suo documento? |
| SERGIO | Eccoli qua. |
| ALBERGATRICE | Eh . . . Grazie. Questa è la chiave della camera, la numero undici al primo piano. |
| SERGIO | Benissimo. Grazie. |

*per questa notte?* for tonight?
*quanto viene?* (literally how much does it come out at?) is
interchangeable with *quant'è?*
*il prezzo* the price
*centoeottomila* 108,000

*esclusa la colazione* breakfast excluded; breakfast included is
*inclusa la colazione*
*posso avere il suo documento?* may I have your document?
*eccoli qua* here they are (referring to the documents, e.g.
passports or identity cards)
*la chiave* the key
*la numero undici* number 11 (*la* refers to *la camera*)

## A single room with shower
**3**

| | |
|---|---|
| GIULIA | Buongiorno. |
| ALBERGATRICE | Buongiorno. |
| GIULIA | Ho prenotato una camera. |
| ALBERGATRICE | Sì. Il suo nome, per cortesia? |
| GIULIA | Puchetti. |
| ALBERGATRICE | Sì, la Signora Puchetti, è una camera singola con la doccia, per due notti. |
| GIULIA | Sì. |
| ALBERGATRICE | Giusto? |
| GIULIA | Sì. |
| ALBERGATRICE | Bene, allora, mi può lasciare il documento? |
| GIULIA | Eccolo qui. |
| ALBERGATRICE | Eh . . . Le dò la chiave, la camera è la numero trentatré al terzo piano. Si può accomodare. |
| GIULIA | Grazie. |
| ALBERGATRICE | Prego. |

*ho prenotato* I have booked
*il suo nome* your name
*per cortesia* please, equivalent of *per favore*
*una camera singola* a single room
*con la doccia* with a shower
*per due notti* for two nights
*giusto?* is that right?
*mi può lasciare il documento?* can you leave me your identity

card (literally document)?
*le dò la chiave* I'll give you the key
*al terzo piano* on the third floor
*si può accomodare* is interchangeable with *si accomodi* please
make yourself at home.

### Exercise 1 ☆ ☐ ☐

You are checking into a hotel; complete the dialogue on the
tape. Here are the details of your reservation:

| NOME | SINGOLA | MATRIMON. CON BAGNO | MATRIMON. CON DOCCIA | NUMERO NOTTI |
|------|---------|---------------------|----------------------|--------------|
| Martini | | | 1 | 3 |
| | | | | |

**4**

| | |
|---|---|
| GIULIA | A che ora è la colazione? |
| ALBERGATRICE | Dalle sette e mezza alle dieci e mezza. |
| GIULIA | E . . . c'è anche un ristorante? |
| ALBERGATRICE | No, non abbiamo il ristorante, però posso consigliarle un ristorante qui vicino molto buono. |

*la colazione* breakfast; lunch is *il pranzo,* and dinner *la cena*
*dalle sette e mezza alle dieci e mezza* from half past seven to half
past ten. From is *da,* and to is *a* but as times are always *le,* e.g.
*le sette, le dieci,* you say *dalle* and *alle.*
*c'è anche un ristorante?* is there also a restaurant?
*però* but
*posso consigliarle* I can recommend to you
*qui vicino* near here

### Exercise 2 ☆ ☐ ☐

*C'è anche . . . ?* The presenter on the tape will prompt you to
ask this question using some of the following words and

expressions for hotel facilities. For example: *C'è anche una terrazza?* Is there also a balcony?

*l'ascensore* the lift
*la televisione* the television
*una vasca da bagno* a bathtub
*la piscina* the swimming-pool
*l'aria condizionata* air conditioning
*la presa di corrente* the power point
*il telefono* the telephone
*una terrazza* a balcony
*il servizio in camera* room service
*i servizi* services, i.e. a toilet and a washbasin

### MAKING A RESERVATION BY PHONE

**5**  (on the telephone)

| | |
|---|---|
| ALBERGATRICE | Leon Bianco, buongiorno. |
| SERGIO | Buongiorno. Vorrei prenotare una camera. |
| ALBERGATRICE | Sì, per quando? |
| SERGIO | Per il 2 giugno. |
| ALBERGATRICE | Un attimo in linea, per cortesia . . . Il 2 giugno, eh, siamo al completo, mi dispiace. |
| SERGIO | Ho capito, grazie. |
| ALBERGATRICE | Prego, buongiorno. |
| SERGIO | Buongiorno. |

*Leon Bianco* is the name of a famous hotel in Padua.
*vorrei prenotare* I would like to book
*per quando?* for when?
*il 2 giugno* June 2nd
*un attimo in linea* hold the line for one moment
*siamo al completo* we're fully booked

**6**

| | |
|---|---|
| SERGIO | Buongiorno. |

| | |
|---|---|
| ALBERGATRICE | Buongiorno. |
| SERGIO | Io vorrei prenotare una camera doppia. |
| ALBERGATRICE | Sì. Per quando? |
| SERGIO | Per dopodomani. |
| ALBERGATRICE | Per dopodomani, dopodomani il 27 di maggio . . . eh . . . sì, posso prenotare una camera doppia. A due letti o matrionale? |
| SERGIO | Eh, matrimoniale, grazie. |
| ALBERGATRICE | Sì, d'accordo. Soltanto per una notte? |
| SERGIO | Per due notti. |
| ALBERGATRICE | Per due notti. E quindi, domenica 27 e lunedì 28 maggio, partenza martedì 29. |
| SERGIO | Certo. |

*io* I
*per dopodomani* for the day after tomorrow; tomorrow is *domani*
*posso* I can
*a due letti* with two beds
*d'accordo* OK, (literally agreed)
*soltanto* only
*per una notte* for one night
*quindi* then, therefore
*domenica 27* Sunday 27th
*lunedì 28* Monday 28th
*maggio* May
*martedì 29* Tuesday 29th
For the remaining days of the week and months of the year, see the *Explanations* section for this unit.

## Exercise 3 ☆
Listen to the recording on the cassette. How much would you pay for a twin room with a shower and breakfast for two? (Transcript on page 101.)

## BOOKING INTO A YOUTH HOSTEL

**7**

STEPHANIE     Scusi, per andare all'ostello della gioventù, per favore?

GIULIA     Vada dritto, la prima strada a destra, la prima porta a sinistra, e là c'è l'ostello della gioventù.

*l'ostello della gioventù* the youth hostel
*la prima porta* the first door
*là* there, (literally in that place)

**8**

| | |
|---|---|
| GIULIA | Buongiorno. |
| IMPIEGATO | Buongiorno. |
| GIULIA | Avete posto per questa notte? |
| IMPIEGATO | Sì, in quanti siete? |
| GIULIA | Siamo due ragazze e un ragazzo. |
| IMPIEGATO | Bene, allora mi servono i vostri passaporti. |
| GIULIA | Sì . . . tenga. |
| IMPIEGATO | Grazie. |
| GIULIA | C'è anche il ristorante? |
| IMPIEGATO | Sì. Il servizio ristorante incomincia alle otto di sera fino alle dieci. |

*avete posto per questa notte?* do you have (any) space for tonight?
*in quanti siete?* how many of you are there?
*siamo due ragazze e un ragazzo* we are two girls and one boy;
*ragazzo* and *ragazza* are used for young people up to the age of 20.
*mi servono i vostri passaporti* I need your passports (literally your passports are useful to me)
*il servizio ristorante* the restaurant service
*incomincia* begins, starts
*alle otto di sera* at 8 o'clock in the evening
*fino* until

## Exercise 4 ☆ □□

Some bookings are being made at a youth hostel. Fill in the register page below specifying how many *ragazze* and how many *ragazzi* are booking in each time. Note that the page bears 4 different times, coinciding with each booking. (Transcript on page 101.)

| 26 MAGGIO | RAGAZZI | RAGAZZE |
|-----------|---------|---------|
|           |         |         |
|           |         |         |
|           |         |         |
|           |         |         |

### BOOKING INTO A CAMP-SITE

**9**

| | |
|---|---|
| MICHELE | Buongiorno. |
| CUSTODE | Buongiorno. |
| MICHELE | C'è posto? |
| CUSTODE | Sì, certo. |
| MICHELE | Allora, siamo cinque persone: due adulti e tre bambini, con una roulotte ed una tenda. |
| CUSTODE | Ho il posto che fa al caso vostro. |
| MICHELE | È all'ombra? |
| CUSTODE | Sì, certo. |
| MICHELE | Molto bene. Eh . . . quanto costa? per quindici giorni? |
| CUSTODE | Quindici giorni ha detto . . . duecentocinquantamila lire. |
| MICHELE | Va bene. Allora lo prendo. Ecco i miei documenti. |
| CUSTODE | Va bene. Glieli dò domani. |
| MICHELE | Grazie. |

*c'è posto?* is there (any) room?
*siamo cinque persone* there are five of us (literally we are five people)
*adulti* adults (sing. *un adulto*)
*tre bambini* three children (sing. *un bambino*)
*una roulotte* a caravan
*una tenda* a tent
*Ho il posto che fa al caso vostro* I have the space which suits your requirements
*È all'ombra?* Is it in the shade?
*ha detto* you said
*lo prendo* I'll take it
*i miei documenti* my documents
*glieli dò domani* I'll give them back to you tomorrow. Don't worry about this form; you will not need to use it yourself.

## Exercise 5 ☆
You make a reservation at a camp-site. Listen to your tape for instructions and answer.

## Exercise 6 ☆ ☐☐
On the cassette, Anna tells you where she will be working next year. Fill in the time-planner in the book with the English place-names. (Transcript on page 101.)

| D I A R I O | |
|---|---|
| GENNAIO | LUGLIO |
| FEBBRAIO | AGOSTO |
| MARZO | SETTEMBRE |
| APRILE | OTTOBRE |
| MAGGIO | NOVEMBRE |
| GIUGNO | DICEMBRE |

## EXPLANATIONS

### DATES

Dates are always masculine in Italian. The first of June is *il primo giugno;* after that, dates are not second, third, fourth, but two, three, etc: *il due giugno, il tre giugno;* you will also hear *il due di giugno, il tre di giugno,* etc.

### DAYS OF THE WEEK

*I giorni della settimana* The days of the week

| | | | |
|---|---|---|---|
| *lunedì* | Monday | *venerdì* | Friday |
| *martedì* | Tuesday | *sabato* | Saturday |
| *mercoledì* | Wednesday | *domenica* | Sunday |
| *giovedì* | Thursday | | |

### MONTHS OF THE YEAR

*I mesi dell'anno* The months of the year

| | | | |
|---|---|---|---|
| *gennaio* | January | *luglio* | July |
| *febbraio* | February | *agosto* | August |
| *marzo* | March | *settembre* | September |
| *aprile* | April | *ottobre* | October |
| *maggio* | May | *novembre* | November |
| *giugno* | June | *dicembre* | December |

### SEASONS

*Le stagioni* The seasons

| | | | |
|---|---|---|---|
| *primavera* | spring | *autunno* | autumn |
| *estate* | summer | *inverno* | winter |

*orario estivo* summer timetable
*orario invernale* winter timetable

*aperto* open
*chiuso* closed
*chiuso per ferie* closed for holidays
*chiuso per turno* weekly closing (day)
*chiuso per lutto* closed for mourning

## *QUANTO?*

*quanto?* how much? takes the gender and number of the words it accompanies: *per quanto?* for how long? *per quante notti?* for how many nights? *per quanti giorni?* for how many days?

## *PER*

*per* indicates duration: *per due notti* for two nights; *per tre giorni* for three days; *per un'ora* for one hour; *per sei mesi* for six months; *per questa notte* for tonight; *per domani* for tomorrow; *per il ventotto di maggio* for the 28th May; *per quando?* for when?; *per* is also used with quantities: *per due persone* for two people

## *DA . . . A*

*da . . . a* from . . . to: *da lunedì a venerdì* from Monday to Friday; *aperto dal lunedì al venerdì* open from Monday to Friday (every week).
*dal . . . al* are used with dates, which are masculine: *dal due al tre di settembre* from the second to the third of September; *dal ventuno di luglio al sei agosto* from the twenty-first of July to the sixth of August.

## *IN QUANTI SIETE?*

*in quanti siete?* how many are you? (2nd person plural form)
*siamo* we are: *siamo tre ragazzi* we are three boys; *siamo in tre* there are three of us, (literally we are three)

*un ragazzo* (pl. *ragazzi*) a boy
*una ragazza* (pl. *ragazze*) a girl
*un bambino* child (masc.)
*una bambina* child (fem.)
*bambini* children
*un adulto* (pl. *adulti*) an adult
*una persona* (pl. *persone*) a person

### HA . . . ?

*ha?* do you have? *ha una camera?* do you have a room?
*avete?* do you (plural) have?
*ce'è . . . ?* is there?; *ci sono . . . ?* are there?; *c'è posto?* is there
any room?; *ci sono bambini?* are there any children?
*c'è* is also used in statements: *c'è posto per oggi* there is room
(for) today

### CON, SENZA

*con* with: *con doccia* with a shower
*senza* without: *senza bagno* without a bath

### WORTH KNOWING

### GETTING A HOTEL ROOM

If you haven't booked in advance, you can get advice from the
ATP and IAT offices already mentioned in the previous
chapter.

*pensione completa* full board
*mezza pensione* half board
*colazione* breakfast
*colazione inclusa* breakfast included
*colazione esclusa* breakfast excluded

*pranzo* is the main meal of the day, generally consumed at lunch time

*cena* is the evening meal and can either be a formal meal or just supper

Hotels are now generally classified according to the international star code, but you still find them classified in first, second and third category: *di prima, seconda e terza categoria*.

*Pensioni* offer more modest accommodation.

*Ostelli della gioventù* have greatly developed in Italy over the past ten years. Every major town has one. They are well-run, cheap and pleasant.

Tourist attractions: museums and art galleries are generally closed on Mondays; for some monuments, however, as well as major exhibitions, you must book your visit in advance. APT offices will generally be able to help you with the bookings.

## CAN YOU GET BY?

**Exercise 1** ☐☐ ☆
"Thirty days hath September . . ." Fill in the blanks with the correct month and then list the months with 31 days *before* you listen to the solution on the cassette (the order of the months is slightly different from that in the English rhyme). (Transcript on page 102.)
Trenta giorni ha n . . . . . . , con a . . . . . . , g . . . . . . e s . . . . . . ; di ventotto ce n'è uno (f . . . . . ); tutti gli altri ne han trentuno.

**Exercise 2** ☆ ☐☐ (answers on the tape only)
How would you say
**a**   A single for the 25th of August?

**b** A double with bathroom for the 2nd, the 3rd and the 4th of July?

**c** A double-bedded room with shower for fifteen days.

**d** Is there room for the 10th of September?

**e** Is it in the shade?

**f** Is there a restaurant?

**g** Do you have room for the day after tomorrow?

**h** We are three girls and two boys.

# 5 EATING OUT

## KEY WORDS AND PHRASES

| | |
|---|---|
| **ci porta . . . ?** | can you bring us? |
| **il menù** | the menu |
| **l'antipasto** | starters |
| **il primo** | the first course |
| **il secondo** | the second course |
| **il contorno** | vegetables or salad |
| **il dolce** | dessert |
| **prendo** | I'll have |
| **mi porti** | bring me |
| **prendiamo** | we'll have |
| **per me** | for me |
| **per . . .** | for . . . |
| **cos'è . . . ?** | what is . . . ? |
| **le piace?** | do you like? |
| **mi piace** | I like |
| **preferisco . . .** | I prefer . . . |
| **niente dolce, grazie** | no dessert, thank you |
| **il conto** | the bill |

**MENU A**

## Ristorante "Al Pero" – Padova

| PIATTI DEL GIORNO | DISHES OF THE DAY |
|---|---|
| *Zuppa di verdura* | vegetable soup |
| *Tagliatelle in brodo* | tagliatelle in broth |
| *Riso al pomodoro* | rice with tomatoes |
| *Spaghetti al ragù* | what we call "spaghetti bolognese" |
| *Spaghetti al tonno* | with tuna fish sauce |
| CONTORNI | SIDE DISHES |
| *Insalata mista* | mixed salad |
| *Insalata verde* | green salad |

**MENU B**

## Ristorante "Da Taparo" – Torreglia

ANTIPASTI

| *Salmone con crostino* | Salmon with hot buttered toast |
|---|---|
| *Prosciutto e melone* | Ham and melon |
| *Antipasto della casa* | The "House" starter |

PRIMI PIATTI

| *Risotto all'ortica* | Nettle risotto |
|---|---|
| *Risotto agli asparagi* | Asparagus risotto |
| *Risotto alla quaglia* | Quail risotto |
| *Bigoli alle salse* | Home-made, thick spaghetti with a choice of sauces |

| | |
|---|---|
| *Gnocchi alle salse* | Small dumplings with a choice of different sauces |
| *Zuppa di asparagi* | Asparagus soup |
| *Pappardelle agli asparagi* | Asparagus pappardelle (a type of pasta) |
| *Pasta e fagioli* | Pasta and bean soup |
| *Tagliatelle alle erbe* | Herb tagliatelle |

### SECONDI PIATTI

| | |
|---|---|
| *Filetto alle erbe* | Fillet of beef with herb sauce |
| *Braciola di vitello* | Veal chop |
| *Braciola di maiale* | Pork chop |
| *Tagliata di manzo* | Boiled beef served with sauces |

## DIALOGUES

### ORDERING PIZZA

**1**

EMANUELA     Ci porta cinque pizze, per favore . . . ? allora . . . una margherita, due ai funghi, una quattro stagioni senza cipolla, e una quattro stagioni con cipolla. Grazie.

*ci porta* will you bring us
*una margherita* is the basic pizza with tomato sauce and cheese
*ai funghi* with mushrooms
*una quattro stagioni* (literally a four seasons) pizza divided into four sections, with four different toppings
*senza cipolla* without onions

## ASKING FOR THE MENU IN A *TRATTORIA*

**2**

| | |
|---|---|
| GIULIA | Buongiorno. |
| CAMERIERE | Buongiorno. |
| GIULIA | Ci porta il menù, per favore? |
| CAMERIERE | Certo . . . Ecco a lei. |
| GIULIA | Grazie . . . E da bere . . . una bottiglia di acqua minerale. |
| CAMERIERE | Gassata o non gassata? |
| GIULIA | Non gassata. |
| CAMERIERE | Bene. |
| GIULIA | Grazie. |

*ci porta il menù?* will you bring us the menu?
*da bere* to drink
*una bottiglia di acqua minerale* a bottle of mineral water
*gassata* sparkling, an alternative to *frizzante; non gassata* still

## ORDERING LUNCH

**3**

| | |
|---|---|
| GIULIA | Allora, un piatto di spaghetti al pomodoro, un risotto di asparagi, un'insalata verde e dei pomodori all'olio. |
| CAMERIERE | Va bene. |

*un piatto di spaghetti* a dish of spaghetti
*al pomodoro* with tomato sauce
*un'insalata verde* lettuce, (literally green salad)
*dei pomodori all'olio* sliced tomatoes dressed in olive oil
There is a list of types of pasta in the *Explanations* section for this unit.

### ASKING FOR THE BILL

**4**

GIULIA      Il conto per favore.
CAMERIERE    Va bene.

*il conto* the bill

**Exercise 1** ☆ ☐☐ (answers on the tape only)
You are ordering lunch in a *trattoria*. Consult Menu A on page 66 for your order.

### ORDERING DINNER

**5**

CAMERIERE      I signori, che cosa prendono?
SIG. BORGHESAN   Come antipasto, prendo un antipasto della casa. E come primo piatto, una zuppa di asparagi, e come secondo prendo un filetto alle erbe . . .

*I signori, che cosa prendono?* What will the gentleman have?
*come antipasto* as a starter
*prendo* I will have
*un antipasto della casa* the restaurant's own special starter (*della casa,* literally of the house, of the restaurant)
*come primo piatto* for the first course; *il primo piatto,* the first course, is often abbreviated to *il primo.*
*una zuppa di asparagi* asparagus soup
*come secondo* for the second course; *il secondo piatto* is also abbreviated to *il secondo.*
*un filetto alle erbe* fillet steak in herb sauce

**6**

MICHELE      Per me invece, del prosciutto e melone, per antipasto; gli gnocchi di patate alle salse, come primo e . . . una braciola di vitello, come secondo . . .

*per me* for me
*invece* (literally instead) on the other hand
*del prosciutto e melone* ham (generally Parma) with melon
*gli gnocchi di patate* potato dumplings
*alle salse* with a choice of different sauces
*una braciola di vitello* a veal chop

**7**

| | |
|---|---|
| CAMERIERE | Un po' di insalata di contorno? |
| SIG. BORGHESAN | Sì. |
| MICHELE | Sì. Per me dell'insalata verde, grazie. |
| CAMERIERE | Prende del vino bianco o del vino rosso? |
| MICHELE | Del vino bianco secco. |
| SIG. BORGHESAN | Bene . . . anch'io del vino bianco secco. |
| CAMERIERE | Abbiamo del vino della casa, ottimo . . . |
| SIG. BORGHESAN | Va molto bene il vostro vino della casa. |
| CAMERIERE | Dell'acqua minerale? |
| MICHELE | Per me dell'acqua minerale gassata. |
| SIG. BORGHESAN | Anche per me. |
| CAMERIERE | Grazie. |

*insalata di contorno* side salad as your accompanying vegetable;
*contorno* is usually any vegetable served with a main course.
*vino della casa* house wine, also the restaurant's own home-
made, or home-bottled wine
*ottimo* excellent
*anche per me* for me, too

**Exercise 2** ☆ □□
Consult Menu B on page 66–7. On the tape, one of the
waiters will say which of the first courses are available today.
Tick them off on the menu. (Transcript on page 102.)

## MAKING CONVERSATION

**8**

| MICHELE | Buon appetito! |
|---|---|
| SIG. BORGHESAN | Buon appetito! |

**9**

| SIG. BORGHESAN | Le piace la braciola di vitello? |
|---|---|
| MICHELE | Molto buona, grazie. E il suo filetto? |
| SIG. BORGHESAN | Buonissimo. |

*le* to you
*le piace?* do you like? (literally does it please to you?) *Le piace la braciola?* Do you like the chop? The reply is *sì, mi piace* yes, I like it.
*molto buona* very good
*buonissimo* excellent

## ORDERING THE DESSERT

**10**

| CAMERIERE | E come dolce, che cosa prendono? Abbiamo una torta alle mele, abbiamo della torta alle mandorle, della torta alla ricotta . . . |
|---|---|
| SIG. BORGHESAN | Prendo una torta alle mele. |
| MICHELE | Per me niente dolce, grazie. Preferisco un caffè. |

*come dolce* for dessert
*torta alle mele* apple tart
*torta alle mandorle* almond cake
*torta alla ricotta* a cake made with ricotta cheese
*niente dolce* no dessert
*preferisco* I prefer

### EXPLANATIONS

## ORDERING A MEAL

*Ci porta . . . ?* Will you bring us . . . ? *ci* means to us
*cosa prendono i signori?* what will the (ladies and) gentlemen
take?, what will you have?
*prendo* I'll have
*prendiamo* we'll have

*per me* for me; *per la signora* for the lady; *per il signore* for the
gentleman

*io* I; *io prendo* I'll have; *io vorrei* I would like

*come primo* for starters
*come secondo* for second course
*come contorno* as a side dish

*cos'è?* what is it? You might want to use this expression to
enquire about the name of a dish you cannot understand: *Cos'è
il baccalà alla vicentina?* what is *baccalà alla vicentina?* It is a fish
dish: cod boiled in oil and milk, a speciality from Vicenza.
Here are other questions you may want to ask:

*è carne?* is it meat?
*è pesce?* is it fish? (beware: *pesce* fish, and not *pesche* peaches!)
*è salato?* is it savoury/salty?
*è dolce?* is it sweet?
*è piccante?* is it spicy?
*è con l'aglio?* does it have garlic?

*sono vegetariano* (masc.)/*sono vegetariana* (fem.) I am vegetarian

*non posso mangiare* I cannot eat; *non posso mangiare carne* I cannot
eat meat; *non posso mangiare cipolla* I cannot eat onion

*le piace?* do you like it? (literally is it agreeable to you?) *le piace
il risotto?* do you like risotto? *le piace la pizza?* do you like pizza?

*mi piace* I like it; *mi piace il risotto* I like risotto
*non mi piace* I don't like it; *non mi piace la cipolla* I don't like
onion

*preferisco* I prefer; *preferisco un caffè* I prefer a coffee

### TYPES OF PASTA

Pasta comes in many different shapes and sizes: short, like
*penne* quills or *tortiglioni;* long, like *spaghetti, tagliatelle,
maccheroni, bigoli* (home-made spaghetti), *fettuccine* (thinner
*tagliatelle*). Pasta for oven-baking includes *lasagne* and
*cannelloni;* meat or cheese-filled pasta includes *tortellini* (with
meat), *tortelloni* (bigger, filled with spinach and ricotta cheese)
and *ravioli* (meat or ham).
Remember! Pasta names are always plural! *le tagliatelle, le
lasagne!* If you say *la lasagna,* it means one sheet of pasta only!

Pasta dishes are served with sauces: *al pomodoro* with tomato
sauce; *al ragù* what we call bolognese sauce; *al pesto* a herby
sauce made with fresh basil, pine-kernel and garlic, a
speciality from Genoa. *Al, alla, ai* refers to the main
ingredients of the sauce: *pizza ai funghi* pizza with
mushrooms. They can also refer to the method of cooking: *al
forno* oven-cooked; *ai ferri* or *alla griglia* grilled; and to the style
of preparation: *pasta e fagioli alla veneta* pasta with beans in the
style of the Veneto region; *saltimbocca alla romana* veal and ham
cooked in the Roman style; *fegato alla veneziana* liver fried in
onion and white wine, in the Venetian style, etc.

### WORTH KNOWING

### PLACES TO EAT

The most expensive kind of restaurant calls itself *un ristorante.*
If you are looking for something cheaper, look for *una*

*trattoria,* a small family restaurant. Sometimes, however, you can find both words together: *ristorante trattoria,* and the price can sometimes be the same as in *un ristorante. Trattorie* generally specialise in regional cooking, so they are worth trying! You can eat more cheaply in *una tavola calda,* a small self-service restaurant, or in *una rosticceria,* generally a high-quality take-away specialising in roast dishes, where it is often possible to eat on the premises. *La pizzeria* is sometimes not the most obviously cheap place to eat!

When eating in *ristoranti* or *trattorie,* avoid the *menù turistico,* the fixed-price meal, and be adventurous and try any *specialità regionale,* a dish typical of a particular region. Italian food is extremely varied, and even if you order a dish with an incomprehensible name, you are likely to eat something tasty!

An Italian meal consists generally of *il primo (piatto)* the first course, a soup, a pasta or rice dish; *il secondo (piatto)* the second course, meat or fish; *il contorno* a side dish of mixed vegetables or salads; *il dolce,* or *il dessert,* a dessert. You also have *l'antipasto* starters, which varies greatly according to the type of cuisine and restaurant: *antipasto di pesce* fish antipasto; in the menu reproduced in this unit, Sig. Borghesan asks for *un antipasto della casa* the 'house' *antipasto.* It is always advisable to try recipes, wine, etc. of the house, if on offer: *vino della casa* house wine; *dolce della casa* house dessert, etc.
*coperto* the cover charge
*la mancia* the tip.

### NON-PASTA DISHES

Rice dishes are typical of Northern Italy; risotto recipes are infinite! *Risotto alla quaglia* quail risotto; *risotto alla milanese* risotto with saffron in the Milanese style; *risotto agli asparagi* asparagus risotto; *risotto ai funghi* mushroom risotto, etc . . .

*Misto* often appears in the names of dishes; *insalata mista* mixed salad; *bollito misto* mixed boiled meats, served with different sauces.

Other types of meat dishes are:

*braciola di maiale* pork chop

*braciola di vitello* veal chop

*cotoletta* cutlet

*filetto* fillet

*bistecca* steak

*pollo* chicken

*faraona* guinea-fowl

*quaglia* quail

*anitra* duck

*galletto* spring chicken

Fish dishes include:

*fritto misto* mixed fried seafood

*trota* trout

*zuppa di pesce* fish soup

*tonno* tuna

*seppie* cuttlefish

*salmone* salmon

*Il contorno* consists generally of vegetables:

*patate fritte* French fries

*patate arroste* roast potatoes

*fagiolini* string beans

*spinaci* spinach

*verdure cotte* mixed boiled vegetables (spinach, fennel, artichoke, etc.)

*Il dolce* is the dessert and includes cakes, mousses, ice creams etc. The word also means 'cake', so you can come across *il dolce della casa,* as well as *la torta della casa.* The difference is that torta only means cake: *la torta alla ricotta* ricotta cheesecake.

*Buon appetito!* Bon appetit!

**Exercise 1** ☐☐
Complete the following puzzle:

(Horizontal)

| 1 | Does not eat meat | 4 | I like |
|---|---|---|---|

(Vertical)

| | | 5 | Sweet |
|---|---|---|---|
| 2 | Salmon is . . . | 6 | They come with the second |
| 3 | Beef is . . . | | course |

|   | 2 |   | 6 |   | 3 |   | 4 |   | 5 |
|---|---|---|---|---|---|---|---|---|---|
| 1 |   |   |   |   |   |   |   |   |   |
|   |   |   |   |   |   |   |   |   |   |
|   |   |   |   |   |   |   |   |   |   |
|   |   |   |   |   |   |   |   |   |   |
|   |   |   |   |   |   |   |   |   |   |
|   |   |   |   |   |   |   |   |   |   |
|   |   |   |   |   |   |   |   |   |   |

**Exercise 2:** ☐☐

**a** one of these places is not meant for eating:
*forno   trattoria   rosticceria   tavola calda*

**b** one of these is not meant to be eaten:
*funghi   pappardelle   verdure   cameriere*

**c** which of these would not be a pasta dish?
*lasagne   bigoli alle salse   tagliatelle al ragù   tagliata di manzo*

**d** which one of these would you not ask the waiter?
*è piccante?   è dolce o secco?   senza cipolla, per favore
Le piace la sua braciola di vitello?*

**e** If you can't eat garlic, which one of these dishes is
definitely safe?
*torta alla ricotta   pizza quattro stagioni   maiale arrosto
pasta al pesto*

## Exercise 3 ☆
*Cos'è . . . ?* You enquire about a dish you have not tried before.

## Exercise 4 ☐ ☆
You are having a business dinner. Consult Menu B on page 66–7, and fill in the parts for both host and client.

| | |
|---|---|
| CAMERIERA | Buonasera. |
| HOST | Good evening. Will you bring us the menu, please? |
| CAMERIERA | Subito . . . eccolo. |
| | (She then returns to take your order) |
| | Cosa prendono? |
| CLIENT | As a starter, I'll have ham and melon. |
| HOST | For me too, please. |
| CAMERIERA | E come primo? |
| CLIENT | I'll have quail risotto. |
| CAMERIERA | È ottimo. E per lei? |
| HOST | For me, asparagus soup. |
| CAMERIERA | E poi? |
| CLIENT | The fillet with herbs – is it spicy? |
| CAMERIERA | No. |
| CLIENT | Then I'll have it. |
| CAMERIERA | Va bene. E per lei? |
| HOST | For me, as a second course . . . a veal chop. |
| CAMERIERA | Bene. Di contorno? |
| CLIENT | A green salad. |
| CAMERIERA | Anche per lei? |
| HOST | No – for me a mixed salad, please. |

# 6 MEETING PEOPLE & DOING BUSINESS

## KEY WORDS AND PHRASES

| | |
|---|---|
| sono . . . | I am . . . |
| vorrei parlare con . . . | I'd like to speak to |
| il direttore | the managing director |
| quando torna? | when does he/she get back? |
| può richiamarmi? | can he/she call me back? |
| pronto? | hello? |
| ho un appuntamento con . . . | I have an appointment with |
| le presento | may I introduce |
| piacere | how do you do? |
| fissare un appuntamento | to arrange an appointment |
| la mia collega | my colleague |
| mia moglie | my wife |
| mio marito | my husband |
| sono occupato | I am busy |
| sono in ritardo | I am late |
| come sta? | how are you? |
| bene | well |
| di dov'è? | where are you from? |
| inglese | English |
| prenotare una macchina | to book a car |
| carta di credito | credit card |
| il nome è . . . | the name is . . . |

## DIALOGUES

### MAKING A PHONE-CALL

**1**

| | |
|---|---|
| SEGRETARIA | Zanetti Group, buongiorno. |
| SIG. GERMANO | Buongiorno. Vorrei parlare con il direttore. |
| SEGRETARIA | Il direttore non è in ufficio. Chi parla? |
| SIG. GERMANO | Sono Attilio Germano, della Lori . . . |

Zanetti Group is the name of the firm/company
*parlare* speak; *vorrei parlare con* I'd like to speak to, (literally with)
*il direttore* the director
*non è* is not; *non è in ufficio* he's not in the office
*chi parla?* lit. who's speaking?
*sono* I am
*della Lori* of Lori's; Lori is the name of Germano's firm (*ditta*);
*della* refers to *la ditta Lori* the firm, Lori.

**2**

| | |
|---|---|
| GERMANO | Quando torna? |
| SEGRETARIA | Può richiamare tra un'ora? |
| SIG. GERMANO | Va bene, grazie. |
| SEGRETARIA | Prego, buongiorno. |
| SIG. GERMANO | Buongiorno. |

*quando torna?* when is he coming back?
*richiamare* to call back; *può richiamare?* can you call back?
*tra un'ora* in an hour's time

**3**

| | |
|---|---|
| SEGRETARIA | Zanetti Group, buongiorno. |
| GERMANO | Buongiorno. Vorrei parlare con il direttore. |
| SEGRETARIA | Mi dispiace, signor Germano, il direttore è occupato. |
| GERMANO | Può richiamarmi? |
| SEGRETARIA | Sì. Mi lascia il suo numero? |
| GERMANO | Sì. Zero sette uno novantuno tredici ottantacinque. |
| SEGRETARIA | Eh . . . scusi . . . può ripetere? |
| GERMANO | Zero sette uno novantuno tredici ottantacinque. |
| SEGRETARIA | La ringrazio molto, buongiorno. |
| GERMANO | Buongiorno. |

*è occupato* he's busy
*può richiamarmi* can he call me back?
*mi lascia* will you leave me
*novantuno* ninety one
*la ringrazio molto* (I) thank you very much

**4**

| | |
|---|---|
| SEGRETARIA | Lori, buongiorno. |
| ZANETTI | Il signor Germano, per favore? |
| SEGRETARIA | Chi devo dire? |
| ZANETTI | Zanetti. |
| SEGRETARIA | Rimanga in linea, per favore. Glielo passo subito. |

*chi devo dire?* who should I say?
*rimanga in linea* hold the line
*glielo passo subito* I'll put him through to you immediately

**Exercise 1** ☆ ☐☐ (answer on the tape only.)
You telephone the Lori company – here is your telephone
number: 044 68 48 16.

**5**

| | |
|---|---|
| SEGRETARIA | Buongiorno. |
| GERMANO | Buongiorno. Sono Attilio Germano, della ditta Lori. Ho un appuntamento con il signor Zanetti. |
| SEGRETARIA | A che ora? |
| GERMANO | Alle cinque. |
| SEGRETARIA | Si accomodi pure. |
| GERMANO | Grazie. |
| SEGRETARIA | Gli dico subito che è arrivato. |

*ho un appuntamento con* I have an appointment with
*Si accomodi pure* do sit down
*gli dico* I'll tell him
*che è arrivato* that you have arrived

**6**

| | |
|---|---|
| ZANETTI | Il signore Germano? |
| GERMANO | Sì. |
| ZANETTI | Eh . . . Sono Zanetti, buongiorno. |
| GERMANO | Piacere. |
| ZANETTI | Le presento la mia collega, la signora Bianchi. |
| GERMANO | Piacere. |

*piacere* how do you do (literally pleasure, my pleasure)
*le presento* may I introduce, (literally I introduce to you)
*la mia collega* my colleague (fem.); *il mio collega* (masc.)

**7**

| | |
|---|---|
| SEGRETARIA | Zanetti Group, buongiorno. |
| GERMANO | Buongiorno. Sono Attilio Germano, vorrei fissare un appuntamento con la signora Bianchi. |
| SEGRETARIA | Attenda un attimo . . . che controllo. Domani pomeriggio va bene? . . . o . . . mercoledì? |

| | |
|---|---|
| GERMANO | Ehm . . . mercoledì sono occupato. Martedì? |
| SEGRETARIA | Martedì pomeriggio . . . va bene. |
| GERMANO | Bene, grazie. |
| SEGRETARIA | A che ora? |
| GERMANO | Verso le tre? |
| SEGRETARIA | Alle tre, va bene. D'accordo. |
| GERMANO | Grazie, buongiorno. |
| SEGRETARIA | Buongiorno. |

*fissare un appuntamento con* . . . to arrange (literally to fix) an appointment with . . .
*attenda un attimo* . . . (please) wait a moment
*che controllo* . . . (literally that I check) while I check
*d'accordo* agreed

## Exercise 2 ☆ ☐ ☐
Here is a page of your diary. Which day can you manage for your appointment with signora Rossi?

| **LUNEDì**<br>Roma – treno 7.45 | **GIOVEDì**<br>Appunt. Lori 11.30 |
|---|---|
| **MARTEDì**<br>Roma | **VENERDì**<br>Pranzo 13.00 |
| **MERCOLEDì**<br>Ritorno treno 15.00<br>Appunt. Zanetti 17.00 | **SABATO**<br>— |

## Exercise 3 ☆ ☐ ☐
Record the following message on Zanetti's *segreteria telefonica* (answering machine) in Italian:
Hello, I am Vivian Stewart, the owner of Stewart Software. I'd like to arrange an appointment with the marketing director. Can he call me back? My number is 02 31 81 82 75. I am in the office tomorrow morning. Thank you, good day.

## MEETING PEOPLE

**8**

| | |
|---|---|
| CRISTINA | La signora Fisher? |
| SIG.RA FISHER | Sì . . . |
| CRISTINA | Sono Cristina Degani, piacere. |
| SIG.RA FISHER | Piacere. |
| CRISTINA | Mi dispiace, sono in ritardo. |
| SIG.RA FISHER | Non importa. Come sta? |
| CRISTINA | Bene, grazie. E lei? |
| SIG.RA FISHER | Molto bene, grazie. |

*mi dispiace* I'm sorry
*sono in ritardo* I'm late
*non importa* (literally it isn't important) it doesn't matter
*come sta?* how are you?
*bene* well; *molto bene* very well
*E lei?* and you?

**9**

| | |
|---|---|
| CRISTINA | Lei è tedesca? |
| SIG.RA FISHER | No, sono inglese. |
| CRISTINA | Parla molto bene l'italiano! |
| SIG.RA FISHER | È molto gentile. |
| CRISTINA | Di dov'è? Di Londra? |
| SIG.RA FISHER | No, sono di Cambridge. E lei? |
| CRISTINA | Sono di Padova. |

*è tedesca?* are you German (fem.)?
*sono inglese* I'm English (masc. and fem.)
*parla molto bene l'italiano* you speak Italian very well
*è molto gentile* you are very kind
*di dov'è* where are you from?
*di Londra* from London

## HIRING A CAR

**10**

| ZANETTI | Buongiorno. |
| IMPIEGATO | Buongiorno. |
| ZANETTI | Vorrei prenotare una macchina. |
| IMPIEGATO | Che tipo di macchina? |
| ZANETTI | Un'utilitaria. |
| IMPIEGATO | Va bene una . . . Fiat Panda? |
| ZANETTI | Va bene. |
| IMPIEGATO | Per quanto tempo? |
| ZANETTI | Una settimana. |
| IMPIEGATO | Che giorno le serve? |
| ZANETTI | Dal 26 maggio. |
| IMPIEGATO | Per sette giorni. |
| ZANETTI | Sì. |
| IMPIEGATO | Costa più o meno centomila lire al giorno. |
| ZANETTI | Va bene. Posso pagare con una carta di credito? |
| IMPIEGATO | Sì, può pagare con qualsiasi carta di credito: American Express, VISA, oppure la nostra carta di credito Hertz. |
| ZANETTI | Grazie. |

*vorrei prenotare una macchina* I would like to book a car
*che tipo di macchina?* what kind of car?
*un'utilitaria* a small car
*per quanto tempo?* for how long?
*una settimana* a week
*che giorno le serve?* what day do you need it for?
*dal 26 maggio* from 26th May
*per sette giorni* for seven days
*più o meno* more or less
*al giorno* per day
*posso pagare con una carta di credito?* may I pay with a credit card?

*con qualsiasi carta di credito* with any credit card
*oppure* or
*la nostra carta* our (credit) card

**11**

| | |
|---|---|
| ZANETTI | Buongiorno. Ho prenotato una macchina. |
| IMPIEGATO | Buongiorno. A che nome? |
| ZANETTI | Zanetti. |
| IMPIEGATO | Ha la patente, per cortesia? |
| ZANETTI | Sì, eccola. |
| IMPIEGATO | Ha la carta di credito? |
| ZANETTI | Sì, la VISA. |
| IMPIEGATO | Molto bene. |

*ho prenotato una macchina* I have booked a car
*a che nome?* under what name?
*ha la patente?* have you got your driving licence?

**Exercise 4** ☆
You hire a car.

**EXPLANATIONS**

### INTRODUCING YOURSELF

*sono* I am: *sono Zanetti* (literally I am Zanetti) my name is
Zanetti; *il nome è* the name is.

### ADDRESSING PEOPLE

**signor, signora, signorina**
*Signor* is used without the article when addressing a man, and
is always followed by the surname: *signor Zanetti, signor
Borghesan*. So, *Buongiorno, signor Borghesan* Hello Mr.
Borghesan.

But, *vorrei parlare con **il** signor Borghesan* I'd like to speak to
Mr. Borghesan. *Signore* is only used without the surname
when addressing somebody you do not know: *scusi, signore?*
excuse me, sir?

*Signora* and *signorina* follow the same rule:

*Buongiorno, signora Bianchi*

*Buonasera, signorina Degani* but *ho un appuntamento con **la**
signora Bianchi, vorrei parlare con **la** signorina Degani.*

Note that *signorina,* although still common as a title and an
address, is used mainly with very young women.

### INTRODUCING OTHER PEOPLE

*Le presento* May I introduce? *Le presento la mia collega* May I
introduce my colleague?

*il direttore* the managing director of a firm
*la ditta* the firm, the company
*il direttore della vendite* the marketing director
*il vice-direttore* the assistant manager
*il titolare, la titolare* (fem.) the owner of the firm
*mio, mia* my
*la mia collega* my collegue (fem.); *il mio collega* (masc.) *il mio
direttore*

To translate 'my' with words defining a close relative, drop *il,
la* etc:

*mio marito* my husband
*mia moglie* my wife
*mio figlio* my son
*mia figlia* my daughter

*piacere* (literally my pleasure) how do you do

### BEING POLITE

*come sta?* how are you?           *sto bene* I am well
*bene* well                        *e lei?* and you?

## DI DOV'È?

*di dov'è?* where are you from?
*sono di . . .* I am from . . . *sono di Torino* I am from Turin; if
you want to say which country you come from, the easiest
way to say that you are English, American, Italian, etc.:
*sono inglese* I am English

*gallese* Welsh                         *francese* French
*scozzese* Scottish                     *canadese* Canadian
*irlandese* Irish

*britannico* (masc.), *britannica* (fem.) British
*tedesco* (masc.), *tedesca* (fem.) German
*italiano* (masc.), *italiana* (fem.) Italian
*americano* (masc.) *americana* (fem.) American
*australiano* (masc.) *australiana* (fem.) Australian

## MAKING APPOINTMENTS

*un appuntamento* an appointment
*fissare un appuntamento* to make an appointment
*vorrei fissare un appuntamento con . . .* I'd like to make an
appointment with . . .
*ho un appuntamento* I have an appointment

## USING THE PHONE

*pronto?* hello?
*chi parla?* who's speaking?
*chi devo dire?* who should I say?
*come si chiama?* what is your name? (literally how are you
called?)
*il nome è . . .* the name is . . .

Here are some answers you might well get when you are
trying to contact somebody:
*è occupato* he is busy; *è occupata* she is busy

*non è in sede* he/she is not at head office
*non è in ufficio* he/she is not in the office
*è fuori* he/she is out

*la segreteria telefonica* the answering machine (NB *segreteria* not *segretaria.*)
*siamo temporaneamente assenti* we are temporarily absent from the office

And here is what you might need to say:
*sono occupato/a* I am busy
*ho un impegno* I am committed/I have a commitment
*non posso* I can't; *giovedì non posso* I can't make it on Thursday
*può richiamarmi?* can he/she call me back?; if you want to ask 'when can I call back?', you say *quando posso richiamare?*
*quando torna?* when does he/she get back?
*mi dispiace, sono in ritardo* I am sorry, I am late

## THE ALPHABET

You will almost certainly have to spell your name when you are in Italy. The spelling in Italian is done using the names of cities, rather than of people or things, as in English: *R come Roma, M come Milano,* etc. Here is the complete list; listen to the tape for the pronunciation of the letters.

A  come Ancona
B  come Bologna
C  come Como
D  come Domodossola
E  come Empoli
F  come Firenze
G  come Genova
H  come Hotel
I  come Imola
J  come Jersey
K  come Kilo
L  come Livorno
M come Milano
N  come Napoli
O  come Otranto
P  come Palermo
Q  come Quaderno (notebook)
R  come Roma
S  come Savona
T  come Torino
U  come Udine
V  come Venezia

W come Washington      Y come York
X ics               Z come Zurigo

## WORTH KNOWING

### TRAVELLING BY CAR

Petrol in Italy is sold by the litre, *al litro*. Ask for *il pieno* if you want to fill the tank; if you want to save money you can pay with coupons, which you can obtain from any branch of the *Automobile Club d'Italia (ACI)*. They will give you any information relevant to your licence, insurance, etc. in connection with Italian law, and they will also carry out emergency breakdown services on any roads.
petrol is *benzina;* lead-free petrol is *benzina senza piombo (verde* green).

Motorways in Italy are *a pagamento* toll roads; you can get a *viacard* a credit card which you can use to pay *al casello* at the tollgate. It can be purchased from any ACI branch, but also from service stations and even tobacconists. The symbol for motorways is a black number, preceded by *A* for *Autostrada,* on a green background.
Main roads are marked by the symbol *SS (strada statale* state road); *tangenziale* or *circonvallazione* is the ring road: *tangenziale est* east-bound ring road; *ovest* west; *nord* north; *sud* south
If you want to hire a car, look for the sign *Autonoleggio* (car hire) at the airport, or at the railway station. The categories of cars vary from firm to firm, but if you want a small car, ask for *un'utilitaria,* or for *un'economica.* You will be given *un contratto* a contract, outlining the general agreement *(le condizioni generali).* To hire a car you need to be 21, and 23 to hire some of the most expensive, or biggest cars. The fee may or may not include IVA *(Imposta sul valore aggiunto,* i.e. VAT).

**Exercise 1** ☐☐

1   In answer to which of the following questions would you
not give your name?

**a**   A che nome?

**b**   Come si chiama?

**c**   Chi parla?

**d**   Chi devo dire?

**e**   Come sta?

2   You are unlikely to go out for dinner with one of the
following:

**a**   titolare

**b**   direttore

**c**   segreteria telefonica

**d**   segretaria

3   Which of the following would you not say when making
an appointment?

**a**   Giovedì non posso.

**b**   Sono in ufficio domani.

**c**   Non è in sede.

**d**   Alle tre ho un impegno.

**Exercise 2** ☆

You arrive late for an appointment.

**Exercise 3** ☆ ☐☐

Listen to the recording of the Hertz employee summarising
the contract, and then fill in the details in the form provided
opposite. (Transcript on page 104.)

| AUTONOLEGGIO | | | |
|---|---|---|---|
| AUTO | N° GIORNI | DATA DAL.... AL.... | TARIFFA £ ........... (IVA esclusa) £ ........... tutto incluso |
|  |  |  |  |

**Exercise 4** ☆
You receive a business call.

# REFERENCE SECTION

The best way to develop a good pronunciation is to listen carefully to the dialogues on the cassettes, to repeat words and phrases, and to do the exercises until you are fluent. This brief guide only deals with the basics of Italian pronunciation.

Vowels in Italian are a little different from English ones; they are more 'open', and have fewer variations than the English ones:

A  sounds like the 'u' in bunk:  *banca, pasta*
E  is like the 'e' in bet:  *va bene, bicchiere*
I   is like the 'ea' in tea:  *vino*
O  is like the 'o' in lot:  *otto*
U  is like the 'oo' in pool:  *una*

Difficult sounds:
C followed by A, O, U or other consonants is a hard sound, as in cut, cat, etc: *cameriere, banca*.
C followed by E or I is soft, like 'ch' in church: *cento, arrivederci, cioccolata*.
CH is a hard sound: *pesche* (peaches)
G is also hard when followed by A, O, U: *albergo,* or by another consonant, *grande;* it is soft when followed by E or I: *Genova, giugno*
GH is a hard sound: *alberghi*.

GL is like 'lli' in million: *luglio, biglietto*.
GN is like 'ni' in onion: *signore, giugno, Gran Bretagna*.

H before a vowel is always mute: *ha, hanno* (pronounced A as
the 'a' in *banca*).
QU is like 'qu' in quick: *quanto, quale*.
Z is either like the 'ts' in cats: *colazione*, or 'ds' as in lads: *zero,
zucchero*.

## STRESS

In many words, stress falls on the last but one syllable:
*passa*por*to, biglietto, stazi*one, etc. but this is not always the
case: *lettera, grazie, tavolo*, etc.
Words that end with an accented vowel must be pronounced
with a strong stress on that vowel:
*caffè, dov'è, città*.

## VERBS

Verbs in this course are taught as part of key-phrases, and not
by themselves, as you can get by without learning them
properly. However, here are some basic ones, in all their
forms, including the familiar *tu* forms which are not taught in
this course:

| being | sono | I am |
|---|---|---|
| | sei | you are (familiar form) |
| | è | he/she/it is; you are (polite forms; *c'è* there is) |
| | siamo | we are |
| | siete | you are (plural) |
| | sono | they are (*ci sono* there are) |

| having | ho | I have |
| | hai | you have (familiar form) |
| | ha | he/she/it has; you have (polite form) |
| | abbiamo | we have |
| | avete | you have (plural) |
| | hanno | they have |

| speaking | parlo | I speak |
| | parli | you speak (familiar form) |
| | parla | he/she speaks; you (polite) speak |
| | parliamo | we speak |
| | parlate | you (plural) speak |
| | parlano | they speak |

Italian does not use the words for 'I', 'you', etc. very often, as the verb forms indicate which person is doing what; you have come across *io* (I) and *lei,* you (polite form). The word for the familiar form of you is *tu*. It is used with family, friends, and people you call by their first name; it would be considered impolite to use it with anybody else, especially with people you have never met before.

## NEGATIVES

To make the verb negative, you only need to put *non* in front of it: *non posso* I can't; *non mi piace* I don't like it; *non ho capito* I haven't understood.

## NUMBERS

| 0 | zero | 11 | undici | 22 | ventidue |
| 1 | uno | 12 | dodici | 23 | ventitré |
| 2 | due | 13 | tredici | 24 | ventiquattro |

| | | |
|---|---|---|
| 3 tre | 14 quattordici | 25 venticinque |
| 4 quattro | 15 quindici | 26 ventisei |
| 5 cinque | 16 sedici | 27 ventisette |
| 6 sei | 17 diciassette | 28 ventotto |
| 7 sette | 18 diciotto | 29 ventinove |
| 8 otto | 19 diciannove | 30 trenta |
| 9 nove | 20 venti | 31 trentuno |
| 10 dieci | 21 ventuno | 32 trentadue |
| | | 33 trentatré |
| | | *etc.* |

| | |
|---|---|
| 40 quaranta | 300 trecento |
| 50 cinquanta | 400 quattrocento |
| 60 sessanta | 500 cinquecento |
| 70 settanta | 600 seicento |
| 80 ottanta | 700 settecento |
| 90 novanta | 800 ottocento |
| 100 cento | 900 novecento |
| 101 centoeuno | 1000 mille |
| 102 centodue | 2000 duemila |
| 200 duecento | 10,000 diecimila |
| | 100,000 centomila |
| | 1,000,000 milione |

## LANGUAGE NOTES

Further and more detailed language notes are to be found in the *Explanations* section of each unit:

| | |
|---|---|
| Masculine and feminine | Unit 1 |

| | |
|---|---|
| *il* and *la* | |
| *del* | |
| plurals | Unit 2 |
| *questo, questa* | |

# KEY TO EXERCISES

## 1 SAYING HELLO AND ORDERING DRINKS

### Exercise 1

*Transcript:*

| | | |
|---|---|---:|
| SERGIO | Allora . . . due più tre . . . | 2+3 |
| DAUGHTER | Cinque. | 5 |
| SERGIO | Tre più tre . . . | 3+3 |
| DAUGHTER | Sei. | 6 |
| SERGIO | Dieci meno cinque . . . | 10–5 |
| DAUGHTER | Cinque. | 5 |
| SERGIO | Cinque più tre . . . | 5+3 |
| DAUGHTER | Otto. | 8 |
| SERGIO | Otto più due . . . | 8+2 |
| DAUGHTER | Dieci. | 10 |
| SERGIO | Due . . . più quattro . . . | 2+4 |
| DAUGHTER | Sei. | 6 |
| SERGIO | Nove più uno . . . | 9+1 |
| DAUGHTER | Dieci. | 10 |
| SERGIO | Uno più uno . . . | 1+1 |
| DAUGHTER | Due. | 2 |

### Exercise 2

*Transcript:*

**a**  Il telefono è nove nove zero zero zero uno zero (9900010).

**b** Se vuole il numero di telefono? Allora, cinque due nove uno uno zero otto (5291108).

**c** Il numero di telefono? Allora: otto due zero nove sette undici (8209711).

### Exercise 4

*Transcript:*

MICHELE      Eh . . . il Brachetto è un vino bianco o rosso?

CAMERIERE      Il Brachetto è un vino rosso dolce.

MICHELE      Ah, bene. Allora, due bicchieri di Brachetto e . . . vino bianco secco?

CAMERIERE      Vino bianco secco . . . potrei darle del Soave.

MICHELE      Bene. Allora, due bicchieri di Brachetto e tre bicchieri di Soave.

| VINO | BIANCO | ROSSO | DOLCE | SECCO |
|---|---|---|---|---|
| Brachetto | | ✓ | ✓ | |
| Soave | ✓ | | | ✓ |

CAN YOU GET BY?

**Exercise 1** Word search

```
U  E  B  S  T  E  I  Z  A  R  G  O  M  P
L  N  U  A  R  P  C  C  D  F  H  A  N  Y
B  U  O  N  G  I  O  R  N  O  A  L  E  S
L  O  N  A  D  F  E  L  P  Q  S  U  I  T
O  L  A  R  T  D  D  S  O  A  F  I  L  R
R  I  S  T  O  P  E  R  F  A  V  O  R  E
Q  P  E  A  N  R  V  O  E  B  B  C  D  I
A  P  R  E  G  O  I  D  Z  Z  F  P  N  U
L  A  A  E  R  I  R  D  O  Z  P  S  V  V
V  L  Z  P  D  R  R  I  A  A  E  Q  P  Q
V  U  E  E  L  O  A  I  C  R  S  V  Z  H
```

**Exercise 2**
Bingo card, 600 *seicento* has
not been called.

**Exercise 3**
1b, 2b, 3c, 4a, 5b.

## 2 SHOPPING

**Exercise 3**
*Transcript:* Abbiamo: eh . . . fragola, limone, pistacchio,
pesca, pera, pompelmo, mirtillo, ananas. Poi abbiamo:
stracciatella, nocciola, cioccolato, yogurt, tiramisù, panna e
vaniglia.
*Translation:* We have: strawberry, lemon, pistachio, peach,
pear, grapefruit, blueberry, pineapple. Then we have: choc-
chip, hazelnut, chocolate, yogurt, *tiramisù* (lit. pick-me-up, a
Venetian sweet), cream and vanilla.
*Key:* yes, he does: pesca and cioccolato.

## CAN YOU GET BY?

**Exercise 2**
*Transcript:* Tremilasettecentocinquanta 3,750 lire
Ottomila lire 8,000 lire
Quattromilanovecinquanta 4,950
Trentamila 30,000
Ventiduemiladuecento lire 22,200 lire.

**Exercise 3**
1b, 2b, 3c, 4c, 5b.

## 3 TRAVELLING AROUND

**Exercise 2**
**a** un'andata per Roma, per favore

**b** due biglietti di andate e ritorno per Napoli in prima classe
**c** Venezia, andata e ritorno, con supplemento rapido

## Exercise 3
*Le cinque e mezza* half past five
*mezzogiorno meno un quarto* a quarter to midday
*l'una e dieci* ten past one
*le dodici e venti* twenty past twelve
*le diciotto e quaranta* eighteen forty
*mezzanotte meno cinque* five to midnight

## Exercise 4
Timetable: the train leaves Milan at 7.55; it arrives at Bologna at 9.42; the connection is at 10.00; it arrives in Florence at 10.46.

**IL RITORNO   DA MILANO-BOLOGNA PER FIREN[ZE]**

**PARTENZA**

| | | | | | | | | | | Exp | | | | | |
|---|---|---|---|---|---|---|---|---|---|---|---|---|---|---|---|
| Milano C.Le  p | 0.15 | | | | | | | | | 7.55 | 8.55 | 9.55 | 10.32 | | 12.45 |
| Bologna     p | 2.59 | 3.37 | 5.07 | 5.42 | 6.00 | 6.08 | 6.52 | 7.42 | 7.54 | 10.00 | 10.42 | 11.42 | 12.42 | 13.27 | 14.14 |

**ARRIVO**

| | | | | | | | | | | | | | | | |
|---|---|---|---|---|---|---|---|---|---|---|---|---|---|---|---|
| Firenze SMN  a | | 4.55 | 6.26 | 6.46 | 7.13 | | 8.27 | 8.47 | 9.06 | 10.46 | 11.46 | 12.46 | 13.46 | 14.32 | |

## CAN YOU GET BY?

## Exercise 1
*Transcript:* Allora, di mattina dalle nove alle dodici e trenta . . . dalle nove alle dodici e trenta. E di pomeriggio, dalle quattordici alle diciannove . . . dalle quattordici alle diciannove.
*Key:* From 14.00 till 19.00.

## Exercise 2
1b, 2c, 3b, 4c.

**Exercise 3**

**A**  L'università
**B**  Piazza Insurrezione
**C**  Piazza delle Erbe

## 4  GETTING SOMEWHERE TO STAY

**Exercise 3**
*Transcript:* Una camera doppia costa centoeunmila lire, esclusa la colazione. Eh, la colazione costa tredicimila lire a persona. Eh, una camera singola costa sessantottomila lire, esclusa la colazione, e . . . tutte le camere hanno i servizi e la doccia. Le camere matrimoniali hanno la vasca da bagno e costano centoeottomila lire, esclusa la colazione.
*Key:* 101,000 lire + 13,000 + 13,000 = 127,000

**Exercise 4**
*Transcript:* due ragazzi e una ragazza; un ragazzo e tre ragazze; tre ragazze e quattro ragazzi; quattro ragazze e due ragazzi.

| 26 MAGGIO | RAGAZZI | RAGAZZE |
|-----------|---------|---------|
|           | 2       | 1       |
|           | 1       | 3       |
|           | 4       | 3       |
|           | 2       | 4       |

**Exercise 6**
*Transcript:* Da gennaio a febbraio, sono a Londra . . .
Da marzo a luglio, sono a Roma per un film . . .
Da agosto a settembre, sono a Venezia . . .
In ottobre, vado in America per due mesi . . .
Torno a Londra in dicembre . . .

### Exercise 1

*Transcript:* Trenta giorni ha novembre, con aprile, giugno e settembre; di ventotto ce n'è uno (febbraio); tutti gli altri ne han trentuno.

*Translation:* Thirty days hath November, with April, June and September; there's one with twenty eight (days) (February); all the others have thirty one (days).

**5 EATING OUT**

### Exercise 2

*Transcript:* Come primo piatto abbiamo; delle pappardelle, agli asparagi freschi. Abbiamo una zuppa, agli asparagi. Ci sono i gnocchi di patate, alle salse; i bigoli – sono gli spaghetti grossi, fatti in casa, alle salse. Ci sono i risotti, agli asparagi, all'ortica, alla quaglia . . .

*Translation:* As first course we have: *pappardelle* (a type of pasta) with fresh asparagus sauce. We have a soup, of asparagus. There are potato *gnocchi* with a choice of different sauces; *bigoli* – they're the thick, home-made spaghetti, with different sauces. There are risottos with asparagus, nettles, quail . . .

### Exercise 1

Here is the solved puzzle.

| | ²P | | ⁶V | | ³C | | ⁴M | | | ⁵D |
|---|---|---|---|---|---|---|---|---|---|---|
| ¹V | E | G | E | T | A | R | I | A | N | O |
| | S | | R | | R | | P | | | L |
| | C | | D | | N | | I | | | C |
| | E | | U | | E | | A | | | E |
| | | | R | | | | C | | | |
| | | | E | | | | E | | | |
| | | | | | | | | | | |

### Exercise 2

**a** forno, **b** cameriere, **c** tagliata di manzo, **d** Le piace la sua braciola di vitello? **e** torta alla ricotta

## 6 MEETING PEOPLE AND DOING BUSINESS

### Exercise 2

*Transcript:* La signora Rossi è libera martedì alle undici, mercoledì alle sedici e trenta e giovedì alle quindici e trenta. Quando le va bene?
*Key:* Giovedì alle quindici e trenta (Thursday at 15.30).

### Exercise 3

*Translation:* Buongiorno. Sono Vivian Stewart. Sono la titolare della ditta Stewart Software. Vorrei fissare un appuntamento con il direttore delle vendite. Può richiamarmi? Il mio numero è zero due . . . tre uno . . . otto uno . . . otto due . . . sette cinque. Sono in ufficio domani mattina. Grazie, buongiorno.

**Exercise 1**
1e, 2c, 3c.

**Exercise 3**
*Transcript:* Ecco. Questo è il contratto. Lei ha noleggiato una macchina dal 15 di agosto fino al 30 di agosto, per quindici giorni, a centomila lire al giorno; è una Fiat Uno, tutto incluso.
*Translation:* Here (it is). This is the contract. You have hired a car from 15 August to 30 August, for fifteen days, at 100,000 lire per day; it's a Fiat Uno, everything included.

| A U T O N O L E G G I O | | | |
|---|---|---|---|
| AUTO | N° GIORNI | DATA | TARIFFA |
| Fiat Uno | 15 | DAL 15/8 | £ ........... (IVA esclusa) |
| | | AL 30/8 | £100,000  tutto incluso |

# WORD LIST

All translations given are as used in this book. Bold type
shows where the stress falls in each word.

Abbreviations: m. = masculine, f. = feminine, sg. =
singular, pl. = plural.

Words given in the form freddo, –a have different endings for
masculine and feminine (see *Explanations* section in Unit 1).

## A

*a*   at, to

*abbiamo*   we have

ac**como**di: s'ac**como**di   please go to, please sit down

l' **acqua** (f.)   water

l' **acqua** mine*rale*   mineral water; *l'acqua* mine**rale**
    *gas***sata** (or *frizzante*)   sparkling mineral water; *l'acqua*
    mine**rale** *non gas***sata** (or *naturale*)   still mineral water

l' *a***dul**to (m.)   adult

l' **ag**lio (m.)   garlic

*ai* (= a + i)   at/to the

*ai funghi*   with mushrooms

*al* (= a + il)   at/to the; *al latte/limone*   with milk/lemon;
    *al semaforo*   at the lights; *al tonno*   with tuna fish sauce

l' *al***ber**go   hotel; *l'albergatore* (m.), *l'albergatrice* (f.)   hotelier

*all'* (= a + l')

*alla* (= a + la)   at/to the, in the style of . . . : *alla quaglia*   with quail; *alla vicentina*   in the style of Vicenza

*alle* (= a + le) (+ time)   at . . .

*allora*   now then

*americano, -a*   American

*anche*   too, also

*andare*   to go: *per andare a . . . ?* the way to . . . ?

*andata*   single: *andata e ritorno* return

l'  *anitra* (f.)   duck

l'  *antipasto* (m.)   starter

*aperto, -a*   open

*appetito*   appetite: *buon appetito* bon appetit

l'  *appuntamento* (m.)   appointment

*arance*   oranges

l'  *aranciata* (f.)   orangeade

l'  *aria condizionata* (f.)   air conditioning

*arrivederci*   goodbye

l'  *arrivo* (m.)   arrival

l'  *ascensore* (m.)   lift

*assenti* (pl.)   absent

*australiano, -a*   Australian

l'  *autobus* (m.)   bus

l'  *autonoleggio* (m.)   car hire

l'  *autostrada* (f.)   motorway

*avete*   do you (pl.) have?

**B**

il  *bagno*   bath

il  *bambino*   child

la  *banca*   bank

il  *bar*   bar

*ba*sta   enough: *ba*sta così?   is that enough? is that all?
*ba*sta, *gra*zie   that's all, thanks
*be*ne   well: *va be*ne   OK, fine; *benissimo*   very well,
    very good
la *ben*zina   petrol
*be*re   to drink: *qual*cosa da bere   something to drink
*bian*co, -a   white
il *bicchie*re   glass
la *biglietteri*a   ticket office
il *biglie*tto   ticket
il *bi*nar*io   platform
la *bi*rra   beer
la *bis*tecca   steak
la *bor*setta   handbag
la *botti*glia   bottle
la *braci*ola   chop
la *brio*che   bun
*bri*tannico, -a   British
*buo*nanotte   goodnight
*buo*nasera   hello, good evening
*buo*ngiorno   hello, good morning
*buon*issimo, -a   excellent
*buo*no, -a   good
il *bu*rro   butter

<hr>

**C**

il *caf*fè   coffee: *il caf*fè *lun*go   weaker black coffee; *il*
    *caf*fè *macchiato*   coffee with a dash of milk
*cam*biare   to change: *po*sso cambiare . . . ?   can I
change . . . ?
il *cam*bio   exchange
la *ca*mera   bedroom
il *cam*peggio   campsite
*cana*dese (m. and f.)   Canadian

*la cantina* wine shop

   *capito* understood: *non ho capito* I haven't understood

*il cappuccino* white coffee with froth on top

*la carne* meat

   *caro, -a* expensive

*la carta di credito* credit card

*la carta telefonica* phone card

*la cartolina* postcard

*la cassa* till, till counter

   *c'è* there is

*il centro* centre: *il centro città* city centre

   *certo* certainly

   *che* that, what, which? *a che ore?* at what time? *da che binario?* from which platform?

   *chi?* who? *chi devo dire?* who shall I say?

*la chiave* key

*il chilo* kilo

   *chiuso, -a* closed

   *ciao* hello, hi, bye

*la cipolla* onion

*la città* city, town

*la classe* class: *prima classe* first class

*la coincidenza* connection

*la colazione* breakfast

*il/ la collega* colleague

   *come* as, like: *come primo* as first course; *come si chiama?* what is your name? (polite form); *come sta?* how are you? (polite form)

   *completo: al completo* fully booked

   *con* with

   *continua* you continue: *continua sempre dritto* you continue straight on (polite form)

*il conto* bill

*il contorno* vegetables or salad

*il* *contratto* contract

*corrente: la presa di corrente* electric point

*cosa* what: *cosa prendono?* what will you have?;
*cos'è?* what is (it)?

*costa* it costs: *quanto costa?* how much does it cost?

*cotto, -a* cooked

*crudo, -a* raw; cured: *prosciutto crudo* cured ham (like
Parma)

**D**

*da* from: *da bere* to drink; *d'accordo* agreed, OK; *da
cinquemila* five thousand (lire) worth

*dal* (= da + il) *binario quattro* from platform (number)
four

*dalle* (da + le) *due* from 2 o'clock

*dei* (= di + i) any, some: *dei gettoni* any, some telephone
tokens

*del* (di + il) any, some: *ha del formaggio?* do you have
any cheese?

*desidera?* may I help you?

*la* *destinazione* destination

*destra* right: *a destra* to the right; *sulla destra* on the
right

*di* of

*la* *diarrea* diarrhoea

*il* *diretto* stopping train

*il* *direttore* the managing director: *il direttore delle vendite*
the marketing director

*dispiace: mi dispiace* I'm sorry

*la* *doccia* shower

*il* *documento* document

*il* *dolce* dessert

*il* *dollaro* dollar

*domani* tomorrow

*dom**e**nica*   Sunday
*d**o**po*   after
*dopod**o**mani*   the day after tomorrow
*d**o**ppia: camera doppia*   twin-bedded room
*d**o**ve?*   where? *dov'è?*   where is?
*dr**i**tto*   straight on
*il du**o**mo*   cathedral

*e*   and
*è*   is
*ecco*   here is . . . : *ecco il caffè*   here is the coffee; *èccoli*
   here they are
*escl**u**sa: IVA escl**u**sa*   VAT excluded
*l' espr**es**so* (m.)   small black coffee
*etto*   100 grams

*fagi**o**li*   beans
*fagio**lini***   string beans
*la farma**ci**a*   chemist shop
*le f**e**rie*   holiday
*chi**u**so per f**e**rie*   holiday closing
*la ferm**a**ta*   bus stop
*la fi**e**ra*   trade fair
*il fil**e**tto*   fillet
*f**i**no*   as far as, to, until: *f**i**no al semaforo*   as far as the lights;
   *f**i**no alle d**u**e*   until 2 o'clock
*firm**a**re*   to sign: *può firm**a**re?*   can you sign?
*fiss**a**re*   to arrange
*il forma**gg**io*   cheese
*il f**o**rno*   oven: *al f**o**rno*   oven-heated
*la fr**a**gola*   strawberry

*francese*   (m. and f.) French
il *francobollo*   stamp
  *fritto, -a*   fried
la *frutta*   fruit
il *fruttivendolo*   fruitseller
  *fumatori: fumatori o non fumatori?*   smoking or non-
    smoking?
  *funghi*   mushrooms
  *fuori*   out, outside: *fuori della stazione*   outside the station

## G

  *gallese* (m. and f.)   Welsh
  *gassata: acqua minerale gassata*   sparkling mineral water
il *gelato*   ice cream
  *gentile*   kind: *è molto gentile*   you (polite form) are very
    kind
il *gettone*   telephone token
il *giorno*   day: *al giorno*   per day
il *giovedì*   Thursday
  *giri*   turn: *giri a sinistra*   turn left
  *giusto?*   is that right?
le *gocce*   drops (medicinal)
la *Gran Bretagna*   Great Britain
  *grazie*   thank you
il *gusto*   flavour

## H

  *ha*   he/she has; you have (polite form): *ha del formaggio?*
    do you have any cheese?
  *ho*   I have: *non ho capito*   I haven't understood

## I

*I*   the (m. pl.)
*ieri*   yesterday
*il*   the (m. sg.)
*l' impegno* (m.)   commitment
*l' impiegato* (m.)   employee
*importa: non importa*   it does not matter
*in*   in
*incluso*   included: *tutto incluso*   everything included
*informazioni*   (pl.) information: *informazioni turistiche*
   tourist information
*l' Inghilterra* (f.)   England
*l' insalata* (f.)   salad
*invece*   instead
*io*   I
*irlandese* (m. and f.)   Irish
*italiano, -a*   Italian

## L

*l'*   the (sg.)
*la*   the (f. sg.)
*là*   there
*lascia: mi lascia il suo numero?*   will you leave me your
   number?
*il latte*   milk: *al latte*   with milk
*le*   the (f. pl.)
*le*   you, to you: *le piace?*   do you like it?
*la lettera*   letter
*il letto*   bed: *una camera a due letti*   a twin-bedded room
*libero, -a*   free
*la limonata*   lemonade
*il limone*   lemon
*la linea*   telephone line: *rimanga in linea*   hold the line

*la* **lira**   lira
*il* **locale**   a train stopping at all stations
*il* **lunedì**   Monday

**M**

*la* **macchina**   car
*la* **macelleria**   butcher's shop
*il* **maiale**   pork
 **mal**: *mal di denti*   toothache; *mal di stomaco*   stomach-ache
*la* **mancia**   tip
 **mangiare**   to eat
*il* **manzo**   beef
 **margherita**: *la pizza margherita*   pizza with tomato sauce
    and mozzarella cheese
*il* **marito**   husband
*il* **martedì**   Tuesday
 **matrimoniale**   a room with a double bed
 **massimo**   maximum: *al massimo di*   for a maximum of
 **me**   me: *per me*   for me
*il* **melone**   melon
 **meno**   less
*il* **menù**   menu
*il* **mercato**   market; *il supermercato*   supermarket
 **mezzanotte**   midnight
 **mezzo**   half: *mezzo chilo*   half a kilo
 **mezzogiorno**   midday
 **mi**   me, to me: *mi dispiace*   I'm sorry; *mi piace*   I like; *mi
lascia il suo numero?*   will you leave me your number?
 **mila**   thousand(s)
 **mille**   a thousand
 **minerale**   mineral
 **mio**   my, mine (m. sg.)
 **misto, -a**   mixed
 **molto**   very

**N**

*il/ la negoziante*   shopkeeper
  *niente*   nothing, no: *niente dolce, grazie*   no dessert, thank
    you
  *no*   no
  *noi*   we, us
  *noleggiato*   hired: *ho noleggiato*   I have hired
*il nome*   name
  *non*   not
*la notte*   night
*il numero*   number: *il numero undici*   (room) number eleven

**O**

  *occupato*   busy: *è occupato*   he's busy
  *oggi*   today
*l' olio* (m.)   oil (olive): *all'olio*   with olive oil
*l' ombra*   shade: *all'ombra*   in the shade
  *oppure*   or
  *ora*   hour, time: *a che ora?*   at what time?; *che ore sono*
    what time is it?
*l' orario* (m.)   timetable, opening hours
*l' ostello* (m.)   hostel: *l'ostello della gioventù*   youth hostel
  *ottimo*   excellent

**P**

*il pacchettino*   airmail parcel: *le faccio un pacchettino?*   shall I
    gift-wrap it?
*il pacchetto*   package, parcel
*il panino*   bread roll
  *parlare*   to speak
*il parmigiano*   parmesan cheese
  *parte*   it leaves: *a che ora parte?*   at what time does it leave?

*la partenza*   departure
*il passaporto*   passport
*la pasta*   pasta, cake
*la pasticceria*   patisserie
*la patente*   driving licence
*la pensione*   small hotel: *mezza pensione*   half-board;
   *pensione completa*   full board
   *per*   for, to: *per cortesia/per favore*   please; *per me*   for me;
      *per Vicenza*   to Vicenza
   *permesso*   excuse me, may I come past/come in?
   *però*   but
*la persona*   person
*la pesca*   peach
*il pesce*   fish
*il pezzo*   piece: *un pezzo di formaggio*   a piece of cheese
   *piace: le piace?*   do you like it?
   *piacere*   how do you do?
*il piano*   floor: *il primo piano*   first floor
*la pianta*   map
*il piatto*   dish: *piatti* (pl.) *del giorno*   dishes of the day
   *piccante*   spicy
   *piccolo, -a*   small, little
*il piombo*   lead: *senza piombo*   lead-free
*la piscina*   swimming pool
   *più*   more, plus
*la pizza*   pizza
*la pizzeria*   pizzeria
   *po': un po'*   a little, *un po' di . . .*   a little (of)
   *poi*   then, anything else?
*il pollo*   chicken
*il pomeriggio*   afternoon
*il pomodoro*   tomato: *al pomodoro*   with tomato
*il pompelmo*   grapefruit
*il portafoglio*   wallet
   *porta: ci porta?*   (will) you bring us?

*po*sso?    can, may I?

il   *po*sto    place, room: *c'è posto?*    is there room?

il   *pra*nzo    lunch, main meal

    *prefe*risco    I prefer

    *pre*go    don't mention it, may I help you?

    *pre*ndo    I'll have: *prendono*    they'll have

    *preno*tato    booked: *ho prenotato*    I have booked

la   *prenotazi*one    booking

il   *pre*zzo    price

il   *pri*mo    the first: *il primo (piatto)*    the first course; *il primo piano*    the first floor

la   *presa di corre*nte    power-point

    *prese*nto: *le presento la mia colle*ga?    (may) I introduce my colleague?

la   *profume*ria    perfumery

    *pro*nto    here is: *pronto/i il caffè*    here is the coffee

    *pro*nto?    hello?

il   *prosci*utto    ham

    *pro*ssimo, -a    next

    *pu*ò    can he/she/you (polite form): *può firmare?*    can you sign?

---

**Q**

---

la   *qua*glia    quail

    *qualc*osa    something: *qualcosa da bere*    something to drink

    *qua*le?    which one?

    *quals*iasi    any

    *qua*ndo?    when?

    *qua*nti?    how many?

    *qua*nto?    how much?: *quanto costa?*    how much does it cost?; *quant'è?*    how much is it?; *quanto viene?*    how much does it come out at?

    *qua*rto: *un quarto*    a quarter: *le due e un quarto*    a quarter past two

*qu*e*sto, -a*   this, this one
*qui*   here
*qui*ndi   then

---

## R

*il raffreddore*   a cold
*la ragazza*   girl
*il ragazzo*   boy
*il rapido*   fast train
   *regionale*   typical of a region
*il resto*   the change
   *richiamare*   to call back
   *ripetere*   to repeat
*il riso*   rice
*il risotto*   risotto
*il ristorante*   restaurant
*il ritardo*   delay: *in ritardo*   late; *sono in ritardo*   I'm late
*il ritorno*   return
   *rosso, -a*   red
*la rosticceria*   a take-away specialising in roast meat
*la roulotte*   caravan

---

## S

   *sai: sai dire?*   can you say?
   *salato, -a*   savoury, salty
*il salmone*   salmon
*la salsa*   sauce
*la salumeria*   cooked meats shop
   *scozzese* (m. and f.)   Scottish
   *scusi?*   excuse me?
*il secondo*   (the) second; the second course
*la sede*   the main office, head office
*la segretaria*   secretary

*la segreteria telefonica*   the answering machine

*il semaforo*   the lights

  *sempre*   always, still: *sempre dritto*   straight on

  *senza*   without

*le seppie* (pl.)   cuttlefish

*la sera*   evening

*il servizio in camera*   room service: *il servizio sveglia*   alarm-call service

  *servono: mi servono i passaporti*   I need your passports

  *sì*   yes

  *siamo*   we are

*il signor . . .*   Mr . . .

*la signora*   lady, Mrs . . .

*il signore*   gentleman

*la signorina*   Miss . . . , young lady

  *singola*   single

  *sinistra*   left: *a sinistra*   to the left

  *soltanto*   only

  *sono*   I am

  *specialità*   a typical dish

*le stagioni*   seasons

  *stamattina*   this morning

*la stanza*   bedroom

*la stazione*   railway station

*la sterlina*   pound sterling

  *storico, -a*   historic

*la strada*   road

  *subito*   immediately

*il suo*   his/her/s; your/yours (polite form)

*il supermercato*   supermarket

*il supplemento*   supplement

**T**

*il* **tabaccaio**   tobacconist
*la* **tavola calda**   self-service restaurant
*il* **tè**   tea
   **tedesco, -a**   German
*il* **telefono**   telephone
*la* **televisione**   television; TV set
   **temporaneamente**   temporarily
*la* **tenda**   tent
*la* **terrazza**   balcony
*il* **tipo**   type
*il/ la* **titolare**   the owner (of the firm)
*la* **toilette**   toilet
*il* **tonno**   tuna fish
   **torna**   he, she comes back: *quando torna?*   when does he
      come back?
*la* **torta**   cake, sweet
   **tra**   *between, within: tra un'ora*   in an hour's time
*la* **trattoria**   small family restaurant
   **troppo**   too, too much
*la* **trota**   trout
   **trovare**   to find
*il* **turno: chiuso per turno**   weekly closing day

**U**

*l'* **ufficio** (m.)   office: *in ufficio*   in the office; *l'ufficio postale*
      post office
   **un'**   a, an (f. sg.)
   **un**   a, an (m. sg.)
   **una**   a, an (f. sg.)
*l'* **utilitaria**   small car

## V

*vada*   go: *vada dritto*   go straight on
la *valigeria*   leather-goods shop
*vede*   you (polite form) see
*vegetariano, -a*   vegetarian
*verde*   green
*verdura*   vegetables
*verso*   at around, towards: *verso le tre*   at around 3 o'clock
il *viaggio*   journey trip
il *vice-direttore*   assistant manager
*vicino, -a*   near
il *vino*   wine
il *vitello*   veal
*volte: tre volte al giorno*   three times a day
*vorrei*   I would like
il *vostro: il vostro vino della casa*   your house wine
*vuole?*   would you like?

## Z

la *zuppa*   soup
lo *zucchero*   sugar

**NOTES**

**N O T E S**

**NOTES**

**NOTES**